Nonviolence Now!

ALSO FROM LANTERN BOOKS

A. Breeze Harper, Editor
Sistah Vegan
Black Female Vegans Speak on Food, Identity, Health, and Society

Kate Lawrence
The Practical Peacemaker
How Simple Living Makes Peace Possible

Ann Madsen
Making Their Own Peace
Twelve Women of Jerusalem

Nonviolence Now!

Living the 1963 Birmingham Campaign's Promise of Peace

Alycee J. Lane

Lantern Books ○ New York
A Division of Booklight Inc.

2015
Lantern Books
128 Second Place
Brooklyn, NY 11231
www.lanternbooks.com

Printed in the United States of America

Library of Congress Cataloging-in-Publication Data

Lane, Alycee J., 1963–
Nonviolence now! : living the 1963 Birmingham campaign's promise of peace / Alycee J. Lane.
pages cm
Includes bibliographical references.
ISBN 978-1-59056-506-3 (pbk. : alk. paper)—ISBN 978-1-59056-507-0 (ebook)
1. Nonviolence—Study and teaching. 2. King, Martin Luther, Jr., 1929-1968—Philosophy. 3. Civil rights movements—Alabama—Birmingham—History—20th century. 4. Social change—United States—Philosophy. 5. African Americans—Civil rights. I. Title.
HM1281.L36 2015
303.6'1097617810904—dc23
2014047204

For my mom and dad, Joan and Ambrose,
who taught us always to speak truth to power
and for Khari, Malik, Lauren, Asha, Miles, and Ambrose III
in whom resides the awesome power of our truths

#contents

#acknowledgments

Many wonderful people knowingly and unknowingly sent me on or carried me along the journey of this book, and for all of them—those named and unnamed—I am eternally grateful.

I thank my editors Kara Davis and Martin Rowe—Kara, for insisting that I write about tactics even though tactics were exactly what I did not want to address (the book is a better one as a result); and Martin, for his meticulous editing and thoughtful suggestions, and most especially for his catching those moments in my manuscript when I was a little less mindful, a little less grounded in compassion.

My deepest gratitude to Reverend Andriette Earl and to Larry Yang, master teachers, whose profound wisdom and transformative teachings have helped me to find the courage to break my heart open and wide enough to write, and to offer this work.

My sanghas, my communities of love and light at Oakland's East Bay Meditation Center and Heart and Soul Center of Light, have been the source of great sustenance and support for my practice. I fully appreciate all of you.

East Bay Meditation Center's Commit to Dharma class of 2012 and most especially Alem, from whom I have learned the great value of spiritual friendship—thank you for your sharing, kindness, and compassion, all of which helped prepare the way for this journey.

Tei Okamoto, who gifted me years ago with *A Testament of Hope* and kept on his bookshelf Thich Nhat Hanh's *Peace Is Every Step*, a book that for me changed everything, absolutely. What a blessing!

Thankful, as always, for the support of my siblings—Ingrid, Ambrose, and Spencer—and particularly Ambrose for characteristically asking challenging and difficult questions that took me back to the drawing board on more than one occasion.

Finally, and most especially, Jennifer B. Lyle—my partner, my heart, who listened, questioned, smirked, laughed, cajoled, held, and loved me through the final chapter and beyond. Without you, this book simply would not have been possible. Thank you.

It is my great hope that as the Negro plunges deeper into the quest for freedom he will plunge even deeper into the philosophy of nonviolence.

—Martin Luther King Jr.[1]

#introduction

The 1963 Birmingham Campaign

The Nonviolent Army

The Birmingham Campaign of 1963 was a pivotal event in the civil rights movement's struggle against racism and racial segregation in the southern United States. As a result of their sustained, community-wide organizing against the segregationist political, economic, and social structure of Birmingham, Alabama, the Alabama Christian Movement for Human Rights (ACMHR) and the Southern Christian Leadership Conference (SCLC)—the organizations that spearheaded the campaign—won concessions from Birmingham leadership that proved to be the death knell for de jure segregation in both Birmingham and in the South generally. Their efforts helped set the stage for the passage of the Civil Rights Act of 1964 and the Voting Rights Act of 1965, two of the most important pieces of civil rights legislation that this nation has adopted to protect and guarantee the rights of African Americans.

The success of the Birmingham Campaign can be attributed in no small measure to the discipline and commitment of those children, women, and men—"the nonviolent army" as they were called—who not only volunteered their time, energy, and material resources to ensure the success of the campaign, but who also put their bodies—indeed, their lives—on the line for freedom. Because they were willing to subject themselves to beatings, the jets from fire hoses, the vicious police-dog attacks, and violent arrests, these volunteers were able to lay bare to the world the racist brutality with which the South was, and had always been, governed.

Through their courage and resolve, the volunteers also demonstrated to the world just how powerful the practice of nonviolent resistance was. Trained rigorously by the SCLC/ACMHR staffs in nonviolent strategies and tactics, the volunteers successfully met without retaliation the hatred and violence visited upon them by angry mobs and law enforcement.

Not all members of the volunteer army, however, were deployed to sit in, march, or engage in acts of civil disobedience that were likely to elicit the white community's retaliation. Indeed, the makings of the nonviolent army involved a disciplined process of preparation through which SCLC/ACMHR staff identified community members who could commit to nonviolent resistance.

As Martin Luther King Jr. described in his 1963 *Why We Can't Wait*, ACMHR and SCLC called nightly mass meetings at African American churches throughout Birmingham to solicit volunteers for the campaign, to motivate and inspire the community, and to provide updates on campaign developments. During these meetings, King would speak "on the philosophy of nonviolence and its methods" and, "toward the end," either he or Ralph Abernathy or Fred Shuttlesworth would "extend an appeal for volunteers to serve" in the nonviolent army. "We made it clear," King wrote, that "we would not send anyone out to demonstrate who had not convinced himself and us that he could accept and endure violence without retaliation."[2]

This initial appeal was of no small matter, for many in the community who sought to participate in the campaign were prepared to defend themselves—with weapons, if necessary—from the anticipated violent response to the demonstrations. "We urged the volunteers to give up any possible weapons that they might have on their persons," wrote King. Moreover, he and the others endeavored "to prove" to the potential volunteers that "they needed no weapons—not so much as a toothpick. We proved that we possessed the most formidable weapon of all—the conviction that we were right." The nonviolent army, King argued, would be one that would "sing but not slay."[3]

Indeed, campaign volunteer James W. Stewart recalled, for instance, that during a mass meeting campaign organizers "asked if we would please put [the weapons] in the basket when it came around, and the basket went around the room and it was empty when it got back. I don't know if it was Dr. King or someone else who spoke to us more assertively, kind of like a minister who didn't get enough money the first time the basket was passed. But he said something to us about the importance of not having weapons, and the next time the basket went around, it was filled with all kinds of weapons that we had which were our personal security. We had to give that up for the greater cause, and we did."[4]

Volunteers like Stewart who were persuaded by the proof that King and the other campaign leaders provided were then invited, at the end of the mass meetings, to meet briefly with the campaign's Leadership Training Committee in order to make an appointment "for screening and intensive training."[5] Thus, even though potential volunteers might have been persuaded by the arguments for nonviolent resistance, the strength of their convictions would nevertheless be tested before they were actually deployed on the front lines.

During these training sessions, for example, staff subjected volunteers to the "sociodramas" that they were likely to encounter during a demonstration. "The harsh language and the physical abuse of the police and the self-appointed guardians of the law," King explained, "were frankly presented, along with the nonviolent creed in action: to resist without bitterness; to be cursed and not reply; to be beaten and not hit back." Not surprisingly, many volunteers were unable to commit to the nonviolent creed when faced with such violence, and were therefore "utilized in one of a dozen other ways to help the cause."[6]

Whether or not they were chosen to participate in the demonstrations, "every volunteer," King wrote, "was required to sign a commitment card"—a pledge, as it were, to dedicate themselves body and soul "to the nonviolent movement."[7] And it is this card—the pledge contained therein—that is the focus of this book.

The Birmingham Campaign Commitment Card

I hereby pledge myself—my person and body—to the nonviolent movement. Therefore I will keep the following ten commandments:

1. MEDITATE daily on the teachings and life of Jesus.
2. REMEMBER always that the nonviolent movement in Birmingham seeks justice and reconciliation—not victory.
3. WALK and TALK in the manner of love, for God is love.
4. PRAY daily to be used by God in order that all men might be free.
5. SACRIFICE personal wishes in order that all men might be free.
6. OBSERVE with both friend and foe the ordinary rules of courtesy.
7. SEEK to perform regular service for others and for the world.
8. REFRAIN from the violence of fist, tongue, or heart.
9. STRIVE to be in good spiritual and bodily health.
10. FOLLOW the directions of the movement and of the captain of a demonstration.

I sign this pledge, having seriously considered what I do and with the determination and will to persevere.

Name
Address
Phone
Nearest Relative
Address

Besides demonstrations, I could also help the movement by: (Circle the proper items)
Run errands, Drive my car, Fix food for volunteers, Clerical work, Make phone calls, Answer phones, Mimeograph, Type, Print signs, Distribute leaflets.

ALABAMA CHRISTIAN MOVEMET FOR HUMAN RIGHTS
BIRMINGHAM Affiliate of S.C.L.C.
505½ North 17th Street
F. L. Shuttlesworth, President[8]

For all of the focus that was and continues to be placed on the Birmingham Campaign's (and, more broadly, on the civil rights movement's) use of nonviolence as a *strategy* and *tactic*, this remarkable pledge actually speaks to the deeper intention by which SCLC and ACMHR were guided. That intention was to facilitate the transformation of African American communities—indeed, America itself—into communities where nonviolence would constitute *a way of life*. To realize this intention, SCLC and ACMHR, through the commandments, encouraged volunteers to dedicate themselves to a life of spiritual contemplation, mindful and compassionate practice at the level of everyday personal interaction, self-love, generosity, humility, selflessness, and, of course, nonviolent political action grounded in love.

Moreover, the card revealed that organizers operated from a conception of freedom and justice that went beyond the desire to dismantle racial segregation and to realize African Americans' full participation in American life. For them, freedom was also the transformation of the self, the excavation from within of violence that manifests not solely as physical aggression, but also as selfishness, a lack of compassion and concern for others, mistreatment of one's body, and disregard for one's spiritual health. In other words, through the commitment card SCLC and ACMHR proclaimed that a free and just society is one manifested by our everyday willingness to "walk and talk in the manner of love." To this end, SCLC and ACMHR sought both the political *and spiritual* liberation of black people and of *all* humanity.

To be sure, SCLC and ACMHR used "the ten commandments" also to reinforce the tactical dimensions of nonviolent protest. As S. Taudin Chabot notes, the "second, third, sixth, eighth, and tenth 'commandments'" in particular "were essential organizational procedures for maintaining discipline during protest events in Birmingham."[9] However, given that SCLC and ACMHR required "every" volunteer to sign the commitment card, they apparently aspired to the community's achievement of something broader—and higher—than discipline and tactics.

The focus on the tactical aspects of nonviolence during the Birmingham Campaign (and beyond) often and eventually overwhelmed the deeper intention that is embedded in the commitment card—an inevitable outcome, no doubt, of the intense violence that protestors faced. In addition to the brutality volunteers suffered during demonstrations, Birmingham's African American community was the target of myriad acts of terrorism, some organized, some not. This terrorism included such acts as shooting into the homes of activists, physically assaulting African Americans, and threatening participants' livelihood. "Every day," recalled volunteer Carrie Delores Hamilton Lock, "there was something to let black people know that they were not safe. [Whites] would intimidate our parents and tell them, 'If you go to these meetings, you're not going to have a job.'"[10]

Indeed, it was during this campaign that the Ku Klux Klan bombed on a Sunday morning in September 1963 Birmingham's Sixteenth Street Baptist Church, and consequently killed Addie Mae Collins, Denise McNair, Carole Robertson, and Cynthia Wesley—four young girls who were preparing to lead church services. To maintain the discipline of nonviolence within this context of terror—many African Americans understandably found the leadership's insistence on nonretaliation taxing—required that movement leadership persistently reinforce its claim that not only did the tactics of nonviolence work, but also that they *were* working.

It was challenging enough for SCLC and ACMHR staff to persuade people willingly and continuously to expose themselves to violence, even if just for a moment. Though making themselves available to brutality must have required from demonstrators a radical rethinking of the self and may have in fact persuaded many to embrace and embody nonviolence as part of their everyday lived experience, it was still a formidable task. Thus, the leadership had to make sure that demonstrators could, throughout the campaign, maintain their discipline of nonretaliation.

Yet, SCLC and ACMHR leadership did not believe that the use of nonviolence as a tactic required practitioners' commitment to nonviolence as a way of life. Although "nonviolence is ultimately a way of life that men live because of the sheer morality of its claim," and in the "truest sense is not a strategy that one uses simply because it is expedient at the moment,"[11] wrote King, for instance, it would nevertheless "be wrong, and even disastrous to demand principled agreement on non-violence as a pre-condition to non-violent action. What is required is the spiritual determination of the people to be true to the principle as it works in this specific action."[12] King's hope, however, was that through the practice of nonviolence, African Americans would be transformed and come to embrace nonviolence as a way of life. As he theorized:

> When Negroes involve themselves in such a struggle, they take a radical step. Their rejection of hatred and oppression in the specific situation cannot be confined to a single issue. For it raises the question of hatred and oppression in the society as a whole,

> it moves toward an even deeper commitment to a pervasive social change. For out of this one problem, the sense of brotherhood springs as a practical necessity, and once this happens, there is revealed the vision of a society of brotherhood. We seek new ways of human beings living together.[13]

For King, the transformative effect of nonviolent practice was itself evidenced by what he claimed had taken place during the 1955 Bus Boycott in Montgomery. "In Montgomery, crime among Negroes declined markedly during the course of the boycott. There was no organized campaign in this direction. What happened was that the very presence of a sense of social mission and human brotherhood worked tremendous changes in the personal lives of those involved. Thus, even when non-violence is accepted as a practical means, an instrument, it has profound spiritual consequences."[14]

Given both the need to ensure that the community would adhere faithfully during the Birmingham Campaign to the practice of nonviolence and the leadership's belief that the strategic use of nonviolence might ultimately awaken African American communities and the nation to the correctness of embracing nonviolence as a way of life, the leadership's failure to engage in a sustained conversation about nonviolence as an everyday practice within the home, with friends, neighbors, and strangers should come as no surprise.

Nonviolence as a way of life was also not something that proponents emphasized during the civil rights movement in general. Consequently, as the stakes for tactical nonviolence rose in the course of the movement (more and more activists began to question the rationale of nonretaliation) the idea of nonviolence as a way of life diminished. What emerged instead were debates on the relevance of nonviolence in the face of persistent white resistance and in the context of armed struggles worldwide to overthrow white colonial rule—not to mention its relevance as an answer to the escalating war in Vietnam. The moment that Student Nonviolent Coordinating Committee (SNCC) chairman Stokely Carmichael—during a 1966 march organized as a continuation of James Meredith's March Against Fear in the immediate aftermath of Meredith's assassination—uttered the words "black power" (a phrase that captured African Americans' frustration with both the pace of change and continued, unapologetic violence from white communities), meant that nonviolence would never be again considered—at least not on a movement-wide basis—outside of the limited framework of strategy and tactics. King, of course, would continue to advocate for this way of life to the day of his assassination.

Nonetheless, the need to embrace the broader vision expressed through the "ten commandments" did not itself diminish, for violence remained a salient feature of everyday life in Birmingham, in African American communities generally, and in the nation as a whole. Domestic violence; crime; the nation's proxy wars in Africa, Asia, and Central America, and the drug wars that were their logical outcome: the arms race and the proliferation of prisons—these spoke to a "deeper malady" (to use King's words), to an acceptance of violence as "just the way that things are," that persists to this day.

Thus, on a nightly basis newscasters blithely recount the day's violence of "fist, tongue, or heart" in the home, in schools, and in the community. Almost without respite we are bombarded, whether over the airwaves or through social media, with the cynical and often hateful discourse of talking heads, whose sole purpose, it seems, is to kill hope and any urge by everyday people to realize justice. Not a day passes when we are not confronted with the consequences of our representatives' choices to pursue the interests of their donors over the need to enact policies that would eradicate the economic violence of unemployment and poverty. Increasing economic and social inequality, the concentration of unimaginable wealth in the hands of a few, the depletion and ruin of Earth's resources, the persistence of racism and sexism, permanent war, climate change—are we not being urgently called to traverse the path to spiritual and political liberation that, fifty years ago, SCLC and ACMHR laid before us?

A New Pledge for the Twenty-first Century

The answer, I believe, is a resounding "Yes!" In the chapters that follow, I offer what I hope will help us to answer that call. Together, they constitute a new pledge to nonviolence, one from which we can transform our own lives and ultimately deepen our commitment to realizing peace and justice.

I begin this book with the Birmingham commitments themselves. As practices that were intended to nurture within campaign volunteers a commitment to a nonviolent way of life, they are an ideal point of departure for our journey as well. I examine the commitments more closely so that we might understand their relationship to the purposes of Birmingham's important civil rights campaign, discern their deeper spiritual meaning and intention, and grasp the lessons that they teach us today about what it means to live nonviolence fully.

I should note that my discussion of these commitments reflects the fact that I take a more secular approach to embracing nonviolence than that offered by SCLC and ACMHR. The Birmingham Campaign was of course steeped in a prophetic and engaged vision of Christianity, as was the civil rights movement generally. Such a vision proved to be a powerful force, one that enabled many to face down fear and, just as critically, to see themselves not merely as a nonviolent army, but as God's soldiers for freedom and justice. Grounded in their Christian faith, then, many volunteers understood themselves to be the instruments by which God bent toward justice "the arc of the moral universe."[15]

However, a commitment to nonviolence as a way of life is not a specifically religious endeavor—a truth that was certainly understood and articulated during the course of both the campaign and the civil rights movement. "I am aware of the fact," King once acknowledged, "that there are persons who believe firmly in nonviolence who do not believe in a personal God."[16] With this awareness, and having taken a page from His Holiness the Dalai Lama's *Beyond Religion*—a treatise in which His Holiness calls for a secular approach to the promotion of "inner values" since "any religion-based answer to the problem of our neglect of inner values can never be universal"[17]—I have examined the Birmingham Campaign card and constructed the new commitments in ways that I hope speak to people of many faiths or of no faith at all.

That being said, I would be remiss if I did not acknowledge that my work is deeply informed by my own personal embrace and practice of Buddhism. Nevertheless, because my aim here is by and large to create a more secular pledge, it is that objective that my Buddhist influences serve. In any event, I invite you to observe the commitments—and indeed, to *modify* them—in ways that work specifically for you.

From my initial discussion of the campaign card I go on to offer five new commitments—Practice forgiveness; Extend compassion, love, and kindness to those who express and act with ill will; Reestablish a connection to Earth; Strive to be in good bodily health; and Cultivate hope—all of which are fully influenced by the Birmingham pledge and yet speak directly to our twenty-first-century concerns. Yet, for my discussion of these new commitments I change gears entirely, for through these commitments (and to a lesser degree, through my analysis of the Birmingham pledge) I attempt to draw out an idea that was left unspoken in the Birmingham Campaign card and yet was, and is, absolutely crucial to the promises contained therein: that in order to live a life of nonviolence, one must be willing to *soften*—to open one's heart to others, to forgive, to be compassionate, to be graceful, to be loving toward others and oneself, to be kind. We must be willing, in other words, to reject hardness as the measure of power and justice, and to embrace, instead, so much of what is commonly associated with the feminine. Indeed, it is no longer tenable—if it ever were—to assess and critique nonviolence in terms of whether or not it conforms to some masculine idea of the justice-seeking self. (This approach, unfortunately, to a great extent drove the debates on strategy and tactics that took place during the course of the civil rights movement, and it continues to have a bearing on these debates today.)

We should instead ask ourselves and converse with each other about whether nonviolence as a way of life—whether love, compassion, and care—is preferable in a world roiled by hatred, injustice, and violence; and we should set out to discover what it might take—what change is required *of* us—to make nonviolence the very basis of our relations with one another, with other sentient beings, and with Earth. I address this question directly in the new commitments: how we engage and what we grapple with daily to transform our hearts and thus align our lives with the imperatives of nonviolence. The commitments, then, are offered as heart work, as challenges that seek to soften and split you wide open.

Although I change gears in my discussion of the new commitments, I nevertheless remain true to what the Birmingham pledge also sought to accomplish: to inspire volunteers always to engage in selfless and dedicated political action. The new commitments proceed, in fact, from my presumption that nonviolence not only requires, but actually *compels* us to act, to confront violence and injustice wherever they manifest, because it is ultimately a way of life that constitutes "eternal hostility to poverty, racism, and militarism"—to *all* systems of subordination and the myriad forms of violence with which these systems are maintained.[18] Nonviolence is *not* a posture; it is a healing confrontation, a loving refusal to cooperate with violence and injustice everywhere, including in our own minds, in our own homes, and in our own communities. It is also, I might add, a commitment that one makes to transforming our society from the bottom up, for it is at the bottom—in the barrios, ghettos, favelas, war-torn places, refugee camps, and on the borders—where the full brunt of injustice is felt. As I suggest, we would do well to include in this idea of the bottom the natural environment and other sentient beings, for both are subject to human violence—war, pollution, food production, resource depletion—on a spectacular scale. Amid such violence, we all suffer and will continue to do so if we don't make a change.

And let me be clear: by "we" I mean *all* of us—every person, every community, every nation in the world. Though I often speak directly to African Americans and from the viewpoint of African American history and culture, I do so with the same spirit that ACMHR and SCLC spoke specifically to campaign volunteers and Birmingham's African American community. That spirit was one of inclusion, of invitation to everyone, with the hope not only that those who were not African American would see that our aspirations and nonviolent movement expressed the ideals of equality, liberty, and justice upon which this nation was founded and to which many throughout the world aspired; but also with the hope that all of humanity would join African Americans and answer the call to nonviolence—as a commitment to freedom the world over and as a principled stand against the spirit of nihilism that the cold war and our weapons of mass destruction embodied. As King often argued, humanity was no longer faced merely with "a choice between violence and nonviolence"; instead, each and every one of us was faced with the choice between "violence or nonexistence." (This remains our choice today, made more urgent, one could argue, by a boundless "war on terror.")[19]

My direct address to African Americans, then, is *always* an open invitation to everyone to embrace and practice nonviolence, and thus to choose life itself, to choose love. Just as importantly, it is also an assertion on my part that African American history and culture are the nation's history and culture, so that to speak about, for example, the legacies of slavery and Jim Crow is to speak about our shared national legacies, by which none of us is untouched and in which all of us are implicated. And since to live nonviolence is consciously and radically to live *not* from a place of Self/Other, but instead from—in King's words—our "total interrelatedness," then the moments when I directly address African Americans can be viewed as, and are indeed intended to be, open-hearted invitations to practice seeing ourselves in one another.

An Experiment in Practice

Finally, it is important I share that my reading of the Birmingham pledge and the new commitments have been shaped, and continue to be shaped, by my own experiment, as it were, with the campaign commitment card.

To give some background: I first encountered the commitment card in 2012 when I read *Why We Can't Wait*, a work in which Martin Luther King Jr. wrote extensively on the Birmingham Campaign evolution.[20] I read this text because I had been immersing myself in King's work as part of an experiment I undertook to blog on political and social issues through the prism of his philosophy of nonviolence.

When I encountered the commitment card I thought of it as nothing more than an interesting detail of the Birmingham Campaign, and this seems to be how it is generally regarded. Rarely has it been mentioned, for example, by scholars and others who have written on the campaign and on the civil rights movement. In retrospect, I find this surprising given that (according to King) volunteers were *required* to sign the pledge before organizers allowed them to participate in demonstrations or even do office work.

It wasn't until May 16, 2013, that I finally took a closer look at the campaign card. On that date, the prisoners held at Guantánamo Bay prison had reached the hundredth day of their hunger strike to protest their indefinite detention—a moral and legal travesty that our government has been carrying out in our name and generally with our permission. Resolved that I would no longer sit back and "watch the Guantánamo fiasco primarily from the sidelines . . . with the passive hope that 'we' would eventually do the right thing," as I wrote in my blog on that day, I remembered the Birmingham Campaign commitment card and struck upon the idea of writing and committing myself to a pledge similar to the one that the campaign volunteers signed. I wrote:

> From this moment on, I pledge to make at least one day out of the week a day of hunger, a day to put my body on the line and suffer with my brothers who clearly would rather die than continue the living hell of Guantánamo Bay imprisonment. Not much focuses the mind (and one's intentions) more than an empty stomach.
>
> And for that day or those days of hunger, I pledge also to act. I will at least do one or all of the following:
>
> 1. Write letters to or call my representatives.
> 2. Attend events/meetings addressing Guantánamo Bay prison.
> 3. Share information about the prison with friends, family, acquaintances, and strangers.
> 4. Where and when appropriate, engage in acts of nonviolent civil disobedience.
> 5. Volunteer at organizations that for years have been seeking justice for detainees.
> 6. Write and agitate and agitate and agitate. . . .
>
> I also pledge to meditate and "walk and talk in the manner of love"—and not just for the days of hunger, but also for the days that follow. And I will not stop until these men are given justice befitting a democracy.[21]

What I had undertaken as primarily an act of solidarity had become much more than I could have imagined. Quite unexpectedly, my pledge sent me on a spiritual journey, and indeed it has become the basis for a radical reexamination of my life and especially of my relationship to violence. True, blogging about political and social issues from the point of view of King's philosophy of nonviolence had certainly started to change and work me in ways that I did not anticipate. As I've been discovering from my exploration of King's work, it is one thing to claim one's belief in nonviolence, but it is a different thing altogether to live it in thought, speech, and deed.

Writing and signing my pledge forced me not only to examine just how committed I was to nonviolence; it also compelled me to ask what changes I was willing to make in order to truly live and embody this philosophy of love. This self-examination in turn made me acutely aware of the power within the Birmingham Campaign commitment card—the potential it had to transform the lives of those who were willing to live every day the commandments contained therein.

It is out of this experience that this book, this twenty-first-century pledge, emerged. My hope is that it will give voice to and make real our intention to transform both ourselves and our world through a committed and disciplined embrace of nonviolence as a way of life.

1 Commandments to Live By

We were instructed from Day 1 that nonviolence was the way, and it still is the way.

—Carlton Reese[1]

Though organizers dubbed them "the ten commandments" (to evoke, of course, the biblical Ten Commandments and thus drive home to volunteers the importance of "keeping" their pledge), the Birmingham Campaign commitments are more than a strict set of rules or codes of conduct to which volunteers were asked to adhere. Rather, they are teachings not only about what nonviolence required of them; they were also lessons about how to live so as to be a real force for change. What they taught was that one must both open one's heart and *have* heart, i.e., persevere, give oneself unconditionally and selflessly to the movement for freedom, for peace, and for justice.

To what degree the campaign volunteers took these lessons to heart I cannot say. What I can say, however, is that they put their lives and livelihoods on the line for freedom. Through their sacrifices the volunteers helped to end once and for all the oppressive system of de jure racial segregation in the South.

1. MEDITATE daily on the teachings and life of Jesus

It's no surprise that the first Birmingham commitment is one in which organizers commanded volunteers to meditate on the teachings and life of Christ. Both ACMHR and SCLC were founded by clergy as specifically Christian-based political organizations, and the church as well as ministers played a central role in the campaign, as they did in the civil rights movement generally.

Furthermore, the fact that this commandment is first reflects just how deeply the campaign leaders believed nonviolence to be a fundamentally Christian philosophy. Indeed, during the course of the campaign they not only taught that nonviolence was expressive of Jesus' life and teaching, but they also offered Jesus as the quintessential model of nonviolence: on the one hand, he challenged Rome by speaking of Jewish oppression under Roman rule; on the other, he confronted the powerful rabbis in his community over their complicity with the state. He did this all through a framework in which he construed God's will as requiring all of us to love and forgive our enemies.[2] More importantly, Jesus practiced what he preached: in his most difficult hour, he willingly and effortlessly forgave—and asked God to forgive—the very people who were responsible for and supported his execution.

Jesus' life and teachings, too, served as the basis from which campaign leaders interpreted nonviolence generally and the campaign specifically as a transformative politics defined from the bottom up. Martin Luther King Jr., for instance—who regularly spoke on the philosophy of nonviolence at the campaign mass meetings—consistently taught that Jesus not only "changed the course of mankind with only the poor and the despised," but that he also championed the needs and hopes of the oppressed.[3]

We can think of the first commandment, then, as one by which organizers encouraged volunteers to follow Jesus' example: i.e., to challenge the powers that be to "change the course of mankind" from a commitment to a bottom-up transformation of society—and to do this by turning the other cheek when faced with violence, forgiving adversaries, and meeting hate with the power of unconditional love.

To Meditate Daily

But how, precisely, were volunteers actually supposed to accomplish this? Clearly, it was not enough for them simply to aspire to Jesus' example, since the point of making the pledge was to "keep . . . the commandments."

No, they had to do more. Campaign leaders asked them to develop a discipline of meditation, to take time out of *every day* for quiet reflection and contemplation. Indeed, by capitalizing the word "meditate," campaign leaders invited volunteers—as I invite us now—to think of meditation as a practice essential to the embrace of nonviolence as a way of life and as preparation for direct action.

It makes great sense that meditation would have this kind of value, for it is a practice that Christ himself regularly undertook. He often withdrew from the business of teaching and healing to savor stillness and to commune with God through prayer.

Meditation and prayer were integral to his philosophy—of love, forgiveness, and nonviolence—as well as to his capacity to speak truth to power.

When we take time out each day for stillness, contemplation, and reflection, we establish the conditions by which we can begin to make ourselves more fully available to the wisdom of forgiveness and love—to a "Christ consciousness" if you will.[4] This is because meditation allows us, on the one hand, to take refuge from the noise around us—noise that is too often filled with the violence of everyday life. On the other hand, meditation helps us to discover a great deal about ourselves, including this salient fact: that, as Joseph Goldstein observes, "all the forces for good and for harm playing out in the world are also right here in our own minds."[5] Anger, violence, love, hate, fear, peace, joy all dance within us. As a result, we find that sometimes we are peace and sometimes we are conflict. Moreover we see our own contributions, however small, to the rage and even, perhaps, the hatred all around us, as well as to injustice.

Since meditation, as Michael Bernard Beckwith writes, "*leads to conscious use of the mind rather than being used by it*,"[6] through it we develop the capacity to cultivate the good as well as to release the harm. Indeed, when we meditate, notes Bonnie Duran, we witness "our own propensities toward self-hate, racism, sexism, homophobia float away" and "see more clearly how these work in others."[7] The result is that we learn to have more compassion for ourselves and for those who are caught in the suffering of anger and violence, and thereby discover the inner resources by which we can free ourselves, and help to free others, from such suffering.

For Nelson Mandela, meditation proved to be a fruitful practice through which he got to know himself during his difficult years in prison. As he wrote in a letter to Winnie Mandela in 1970 when she was sent to prison in Kroonstad, South Africa:

> You may find that the cell is an ideal place to learn to know yourself, to search realistically and regularly the processes of your own mind and feelings. In judging our progress as individuals we tend to concentrate on external factors such as one's social position, influence and popularity, wealth and standard of education . . . but internal factors may be even more crucial in assessing one's development as a human being: honesty, sincerity, simplicity, humility, purity, generosity, absence of vanity, readiness to serve your fellow men—qualities within the reach of every soul—are the foundation of one's spiritual life . . . at least, if for nothing else, the cell gives you the opportunity to look daily into your entire conduct to overcome the bad and develop whatever is good in you. Regular meditation, say of about 15 minutes a day before you turn in, can be fruitful in this regard. You may find it difficult at first to pinpoint the negative factors in your life, but the tenth attempt may reap rich rewards. Never forget that a saint is a sinner that keeps on trying.[8]

Our New Commitment

Ultimately, we can consider meditation a practice that constitutes *resistance* to the myriad ways that we are discouraged in our society from tuning out the noise and tuning into ourselves, from developing both the clarity of mind and the softness of heart that are sorely needed in order for us to address injustice effectively and create the conditions for peace.

Let us, therefore, take our cue from the campaign card's first commitment and adopt the practice of meditation for our own journey. As did Nelson Mandela through the years of his incarceration, we can surely take out fifteen minutes a day to sit in silence, to meditate on the teachings of those who inspire us, or simply to focus the mind. With great perseverance, we sit, we go within. Then we follow the example of Jesus and many others by challenging those who perpetrate injustice, and by dedicating ourselves to transforming our society from the bottom up—all from our commitment to nonviolence as a way of life.

2. REMEMBER always that the nonviolent movement in Birmingham seeks justice and reconciliation—not victory

Easily one of the more *exacting* commitments of the campaign's pledge card, this second commandment in effect required that volunteers promise to regard Birmingham's white community *not* as their enemy, but as their partner in the creation of a new and just Birmingham. They were to adopt, in other words, a spirit of reconciliation, to consider any victory over segregation a triumph "for good will in all men, white and Negro"—in spite of the fact that they were subjected to the white community's brutal disregard.[9]

What did this mean in terms of practice? I would suggest that the commitment tasked volunteers to do, over and over again, the tough work of resisting—in their thoughts, words, and deeds—the "us" versus "them" logic of violence, war, racism, and segregation itself. They were challenged to root out whatever violence they themselves might have harbored in their minds and hearts. They were asked to see (or perhaps remember) themselves *in* the white women, children, and men whom they encountered so they could see the fundamental humanity in the very people who denied their own. They were tasked, in other words, to soften their hearts so that they could include whites in their vision of Beloved Community even as they demanded that whites transform themselves in ways that such a community required.

This practice, then, pushed volunteers to go beyond their comfort zone. More importantly, it prodded them to define justice broadly precisely since true reconciliation heals the entire community; it proceeds from the understanding that injustice harms everyone, including those who benefit from its existence.

Radical Reconciliation

We, too, are charged with taking on the challenge of reconciliation, even though it may so clearly go against the grain. Politicians, corporate interests, the media, and a host of others invested in the status quo of division and discord regularly encourage us to see the world in terms of "us" versus "them," to engage each other from a place of distrust, and to pursue our own interests at others' expense.

One need only look at our broken national politics to see this truth in action. As I write, our deadlocked Congress has recessed for the summer, having failed to pass any legislation this year to address such critical issues as immigration reform, unemployment, climate change, the repair of our infrastructure, or any number of concerns that desperately need our mindful attention. Congress, of course, reflects our own unwillingness to meet one another half way, for we are the ones who sent them to Washington to represent us in the first place. In the meantime, people go hungry, the sea continues to warm and rise, and despair has settled into many communities across the nation.

We see this reality played out further in our nation's continued investment in racism, institutional or otherwise. It is laid bare in such moments as the senseless murders of Trayvon Martin, Aiyana Stanley-Jones, Michael Brown, Yvette Smith, Eric Garner, Tamir Rice, and other "suspect" black children, women, and men; the assault on voting rights—from the U.S. Supreme Court to state assemblies; the unprecedented attacks on a sitting U.S. president; the exponential increase of men of color in our prison population; the war on terror; and the resistance to children's safe passage across Southwestern borders.[10] When we should be talking honestly and with integrity about reconciliation and reparations, we instead have to contend with nostalgia for the institution of slavery.[11]

We pursue reconciliation, then, not only so that we can heal the rifts and correct the injustices that are tearing us apart, but so we can get to the point, as Allan Aubrey Boesak advises, "where we learn to live, not just *with* the other—because we have no choice—but *for* the other—because that *is* our choice—where the peace among us is not just the absence of violence but the active presence of justice. When reconciliation is all of these," Boesak continues, "it is salvation: being saved from the lust for power, the lure of greed, the arrogance of self-aggrandizement, and the hard-heartedness of self-gratification."[12] Let us make no mistake about it: when reconciliation "is all of these," it is absolutely radical in its dimensions, for it is an affront to the status quo of permanent division and discord, as well as to the injustices from which these have sprung.

Our New Commitment

We, therefore, pledge *to remember always to seek justice and reconciliation—not victory*, and we remember this by approaching every conflict, starting with those in our personal lives, with the intention to hold and to honor one another's humanity as well as to define justice in terms of healing and wholeness within the family, community, and nation. Just as a "reconciled, restored community is not possible" without justice,[13] so, notes Boesak, is justice impossible if "our broken relationships with the community, with the other" are not restored.[14]

As we take up this pledge, let us also remember Desmond Tutu's important observation: "[B]eing reconciled to our enemies or our loved ones are [*sic*] not about pretending that things are other than they are. True reconciliation exposes the awfulness, the abuse, the hurt, the truth. It could even sometimes make things worse. It is a risky undertaking but in the end it is worthwhile, because in the end only an honest confrontation with reality can bring real healing. Superficial reconciliation can bring only superficial healing."[15]

3. WALK and TALK in the manner of love, for God is love

"At the center of nonviolence," explained King on several occasions, "stands the principle of love."[16] Thus, with this Birmingham Campaign commitment organizers asked volunteers to practice fully the very essence of nonviolence—indeed, to align their acts and speech with the divine, since love (as organizers believed) is God itself.

What is so interesting about this commitment is that campaign organizers had very different images of God from which to choose and to offer as models for volunteers to emulate. For example, organizers could very well have fashioned commitments in keeping with God as retribution, God as war, and even, perhaps, God as arbitrary, gratuitous violence (Job's story specifically comes to mind).

But such an image of God was (and is) truly incapable of being reconciled with nonviolence, and it would have entirely undercut the thrust of the previous commitment. After all, a god of love, as opposed to a god of war or vengeance or gratuitous violence, is a god who reconciles, who embraces, and who excludes no one from its loving embrace. Furthermore, the violent images of God from the Old Testament clashed with the organizers' conflation of nonviolence with the teachings and life of Jesus. "Turn the other cheek" hardly squares with retributive justice.

Viewed from this point of view, the commitment to walk and talk in the manner of love asked volunteers to reject altogether any image of God steeped in violence. It encouraged them to walk and talk against the logic of domination embedded in the God of violence and retribution, since many in positions of power had employed that logic to appropriate *that* god to secure and rationalize their domination and control.

Such a situation was certainly true in Birmingham (and in the South generally), where the powerful—including many of its white clergy—construed segregation as God's will. *Their* segregationist god only could have been a god of violence, aligned as it was with racial subordination, and *that* god, in the end, was one that volunteers also needed to meet with nonviolent resistance—that is, with their god of love. "On Sunday morning, we were going to the eleven o'clock service at a white church," recalled campaign volunteer LaVerne Revis Martin. "When we got up the steps of the church, there was a well-dressed white gentleman who came to the door. We were well dressed, too. He said, 'We're segregated here.' He couldn't even pronounce the word. He wouldn't let us in, so we didn't do anything. We just turned around and left. That's the way we were instructed to do."[17]

Our New Commitment

Embracing the spirit of the third commitment, we pledge to *walk and talk in the manner of love*, for to do so—as the original commitment suggests—is to refuse to participate in our society's deification of violence, militarism, and injustice. It is also to model an alternative order, to demonstrate by word and deed that another way of being is possible, desirable, and just.

In order to actualize this pledge, we can commit, for instance, to speaking out when those in power (or *anyone*, for that matter) cloak violence and injustice—the death penalty, drone strikes, gun ownership, the pursuit of policies that harm the most vulnerable, or the so-called war on terror are a few examples—with religiosity, rationalizing both as ordained by some higher power. When we speak, we do so, first of all, with the intent to expose this mystification and thus reveal violence and injustice as being nothing less than *human* harms. We also speak in order to champion nonviolence as a matter of policy and ethical conduct.

But we also commit to being "love in action" in our daily lives—at home, at work, while driving on the freeway, and when shopping at the grocery store. Since the deification of violence in our society has left no place untouched, love is needed everywhere and in all encounters. This need is one that we pledge to fulfill. So we practice always, in every area of our lives, walking and talking in the manner of love.

4. PRAY daily to be used by God in order that all men might be free

With this fourth commitment campaign organizers returned to the spirit of the first pledge. Once again, they tasked volunteers to take time out daily for quiet reflection. In the fourth, of course, they emphasized the practice of prayer instead of meditation.

This particular difference is not the most important or

even the most interesting variation between the two. When we look closely at the fourth commitment, it becomes clear that organizers used it to *internationalize* the Birmingham Campaign. That is to say, through their use of the words "that all men might be free," organizers situated the campaign squarely within liberation movements that were underway throughout the world, movements that they believed expressed the greater aspirations of African Americans and even of the campaign itself. "Oppressed people," wrote King in his "Letter from a Birmingham City Jail,"

> cannot remain oppressed forever. The urge for freedom will eventually come. This is what happened to the American Negro. Something within has reminded him of his birthright of freedom; something without has reminded him that he can gain it. Consciously and unconsciously, he has been swept in by what the Germans call the *Zeitgeist*, and with his black brothers of Africa, and his brown and yellow brothers of Asia, South America and the Caribbean, he is moving with a sense of cosmic urgency toward the promised land of racial justice.[18]

With this fourth commitment, therefore, organizers provided a framework through which volunteers would be able to see themselves and their participation in the campaign as part of a worldwide freedom movement of oppressed people. They would also understand that a life committed to nonviolence is a life dedicated to the liberation of all.

In keeping with their belief that nonviolence was Christianity in action, organizers also positioned the campaign *and* the broader liberation movements firmly within what they believed to be God's plan to free "all men." Here, then, they encouraged volunteers to embrace the campaign as something that fulfilled God's purpose and that consequently required them to offer their absolute and *selfless* dedication to nonviolence, to the campaign, and to other liberation struggles.

Our New Commitment

Viewed in this light, the daily practice of prayer was clearly intended as a *radical* practice. It was offered as one through which volunteers would be able to transform themselves into global citizens who would work for the benefit and liberation of all.

For our commitment to nonviolence, we, too, dedicate ourselves to the freedom of all children, women, and men—from Syria to North Korea, from Gaza to the Congo. As compelling as our challenges are here at home, we cannot turn away from others' suffering. We are truly connected to others on a global scale, and too often in ways that cause harm. Whether through our neoliberal trade policies, which have decimated the livelihoods of many small farmers in poor countries; our borderless war on terror; our support of regimes that do great violence to their people; or our penchant for mind-altering substances, we cannot take cover under our domestic concerns and think that what we do the world over has no effect on us politically, economically, spiritually. To do so is both dangerous and unjust.

We might, then, promise *to practice a daily ritual of dedication to the liberation of all children, women, and men.* Through ritual, we regularly remind ourselves—against all of the forces in our lives that encourage us to forget—of our connection to one another. Moreover, we reinforce our understanding that a pledge to nonviolence as a way of life does not stop at national borders, as the original commitment makes clear. In fact, it defies national identity as such, if for no other reason than that neither love nor violence knows the fiction of national boundaries. As King suggested in his crucial speech on the Vietnam War,

> Every nation must now develop an overriding loyalty to mankind as a whole in order to preserve the best in their individual societies. This call for a world-wide fellowship that lifts neighborly concern beyond one's tribe, race, class and nation is in reality a call for an all-embracing love for all men. This oft-misunderstood and misinterpreted concept—so readily dismissed by the Nietzsches of the world as a weak and cowardly force—has now become an absolute necessity for the survival of man.[19]

Just as importantly, we can use ritual to unbind ourselves from the inadvertent and not-so-inadvertent ways that we support injustices abroad. If we truly dedicate our lives to the liberation of all children, women and men, then we cannot, as Boesak argues, "claim innocence" regarding "the consequences of [our] political, social, and economic decisions" simply because "the innocence and the consequences happen to benefit us." We, therefore, turn a loving, critical eye on how we live and how our political as well as economic choices affect others. In this way, we can remake ourselves into global agents of change, justice, and peace and thus build what Boesak calls a "canopy of hope for the children of the world."[20]

With what rituals will you dedicate your life to the freedom of all? Perhaps you'll "pray daily to be used by God in order that all men might be free" or develop a meditation mantra or take the time to read something every day that keeps you in touch with others' yearning for freedom. Perhaps you'll fast once a week or burn a candle first thing in the morning to express your wish that all children, women, and men be free. Whatever you choose, pour yourself completely—as if in prayer—into your ritual and let it move you to take action to secure the freedom of all.

5. SACRIFICE personal wishes in order that all men might be free

Whereas this commandment restates the challenge in the fourth to offer dedicated, selfless service for the freedom of all, it also presented to volunteers an additional challenge: to look within, to examine their self-interest or "personal wishes," *and then to let them go*—at least insofar as their self-interests undercut their full commitment to the campaign, to the nonviolent movement, and to the liberation of all oppressed people.

Through this difference, organizers suggested that although it is crucial for volunteers to pray and to call on God to help them become dedicated servants of the movement, they nevertheless needed to do their own work, i.e., take responsibility for changing their personal priorities for freedom's sake.

That the campaign organizers repeated in this commitment the words "in order that all men might be free" illustrates just how important they felt it was to align the campaign with liberation movements elsewhere. We can conclude from this, I would argue, that they intended this fifth commitment—if not *all* of the commitments—to be a radical undertaking as well. It certainly had that potential. By sacrificing personal wishes, volunteers would have removed from their path any and all obstacles that blocked their full, selfless dedication to dismantling segregation as well as other systems of domination, both here and abroad. Indeed, they would have been exercising precisely the "kind of dangerous unselfishness" that King would, in his final sermon, invite us all "to develop" in order to defeat "the evils" of "poverty, racism, and militarism."[21]

Our New Commitment

The practice of dangerous unselfishness is part of what makes nonviolence such a powerful life philosophy. Through it we hold sacred the needs of others and reject the self-centeredness and self-absorption that allow injustice to thrive. What we come to realize is that when we sacrifice personal wishes so that all might be free, we do not actually lose anything—and certainly nothing worth holding onto in the first instance. In fact, we secure our own freedom when we dedicate ourselves to securing the freedom of others. Thus, as we pursue a life committed to nonviolence, we include this pledge *to sacrifice personal wishes so that all children, women, and men might be free*, and thus take up the challenge that King left us with in his final days.

6. OBSERVE with both friend and foe the ordinary rules of courtesy

In addition to driving home to volunteers just how necessary it is for them to *refrain* from doing harm (this they conveyed explicitly in the eighth commitment), organizers underscored the equal importance of volunteers *extending* themselves nonviolently: to exercise gentleness and kindness in their personal interactions with others. The practice of courtesy provided volunteers with the opportunity to fulfill this challenge.

Courtesy was not to be understood as merely the expression of polite niceties (which, quite frankly, are too often bereft of genuine concern for others and can function as a veneer for profound hostility and even hate). Instead, courtesy was to be understood as the kind of personal engagement by which one announces by word and deed that one recognizes and honors another. Courtesy is also a means by which one proclaims one's readiness and willingness to establish a relationship of mutual respect, if not genuine friendship.

We should be clear that organizers did not ask volunteers to be courteous to their friends only. Instead, they tasked them to be courteous to their antagonists as well, and in the context of the campaign this implicitly included the very people who attacked and terrorized them. From this we can surmise that organizers considered courtesy integral to reconciliation and thus to making the entire community whole. Such a position makes great sense: by extending courtesy to one's foes, one demonstrates a willingness to resolve all conflicts on the basis of respect and care for the concerns of others. For this reason, campaign organizers included courtesy as part of volunteers' practice of nonviolence at home *and* on the front lines of the movement.

Our New Commitment

In our own context, it is not hard to see just how much this sixth commitment is needed. Our civil discourse, for example, has deteriorated significantly over the last few decades, such that rudeness and outright hate speech have become the norm. I would argue that this decline has been driven, to a great extent, by the unwillingness of those of us who have been historically marginalized to stay in our place. For some people, our refusal has not been a welcome development; indeed, it has often been met with bitterness, resentment, and, at times, violence. To practice courtesy in this context, therefore, is to confront this aggression *not* in kind, but instead from an ethic of and commitment to nonviolence.

As was true for the Birmingham Campaign, courtesy does not demand that we refrain from speaking difficult truths or from expressing outrage. Indeed, truth is never served if it is stifled or muted for the sake of empty gestures of politeness, or to protect others from what they desperately need to hear or to let others off the hook when they speak and act from a spirit of animus. (This is often what those who call for so-called civil discourse hope to secure, i.e., freedom from responsibility for their beautifully spoken hostility.) Courtesy simply requires that we extend to both friends and "foes" our respectful regard, in our speech and our acts. One can think of such courtesy as the etiquette of nonviolence. As such, we should pledge always to observe the ordinary rules of courtesy with everyone.

7. SEEK to perform regular service for others and for the world

Whereas the need for volunteers to practice generosity was implied in many of the commitments, if not in the overall pledge—to commit one's "person and body to the nonviolent movement" is, after all, generosity par excellence—the seventh commitment articulates the command more directly. Specifically, it asked volunteers to search for opportunities outside of and beyond the campaign to serve everyone ("the world"), and not only those who had yet to secure their freedom. In a sense, this commitment asked volunteers to see the campaign pledge as their promise to serve all of humankind, or, in the words of volunteer Nims E. Gay, to "stand on right and reach out and touch somebody's life."[22]

We might also look at this commitment as one that offered to volunteers a way of being in the world that would constitute a repudiation of the logic of service that underlay both segregation and white supremacy, and in the process expose the moral bankruptcy of both. Both segregation and white supremacy construed (and construe) white communities as communities to be served by others, *not* on the basis of a shared humanity but as a matter of right. The pledge offers an entirely different notion of service, one grounded in care and concern for, as well as commitment to, the well-being of others. From this viewpoint, service would itself be a form of resistance, another means by which volunteers could nonviolently confront the established order.

Our New Commitment

For our own journey, the commitment of service is one that can help us to meet the challenge that was posed by Boesak, namely, that we must "learn to live, not just *with* the other . . . but *for* the other." We learn to live for the other precisely *by doing for the other*, by availing others of our time as well as our spiritual and material resources—by actively seeking out ways, that is, to help one another. It is a practice that continues to be contrary to the established order, for it repudiates the systems of subordination that continue to drive our social, political, and economic arrangements and that define some as "deserving" and others as not.

Moreover, doing for others is a practice that demonstrates, in a most profound way, that there are all kinds of quiet methods by which to practice nonviolent resistance. It is not something that we reserve solely—or even primarily—for the spectacular or momentous occasion. When we take on nonviolence as a way of life, when we live it and breathe it, we find that we integrate resistance even into the mundanity of our everyday lives.

8. REFRAIN from the violence of fist, tongue, or heart

Although we often tend to focus on the strength and discipline that it took for civil rights activists—whether in Birmingham or elsewhere—to refrain from physical retaliation, their ability to refrain from exercising verbal/oral and even spiritual retaliation ("tongue" and "heart") took great fortitude and discipline as well, and was itself the result of training and practice. Campaign organizers put volunteers through the paces not only by physically challenging them, but by hurling insults and subjecting them to other forms of simulated nonphysical violence. At the same time, they taught volunteers how important it was to love even those who "spitefully use you."

When we look at film footage of the Birmingham Campaign demonstrations (especially the lunch counter sit-ins), what we see before us is not only volunteers' refusal to retaliate physically; we see also their refusal to engage in the violence of tongue, and even, perhaps, heart. "I went to Woolworth's," recalls volunteer LaVerne Revis Martin, "and sat at the lunch counter, when a white gentleman coughed and spat in the face of the man next to me. The man next to me smiled and didn't retaliate. He was nonviolent and did what we were supposed to do."[23] If it is true that during these terrible moments the volunteers harbored in their hearts ill will for their assailants, we can surmise that at the very least, their ill will was hardly enough to compel them to "spit" back as it were. (What fortitude of spirit, I wonder, enables someone to "smile" at such a hateful physical and spiritual assault?) Of all the commitments, this was the one that organizers made volunteers practice. Not only did they reinforce the commitment through civil disobedience trainings; they enforced it during the course of demonstrations.

You will notice that this eighth commitment is not limited in scope. Organizers did not ask volunteers, for instance, to refrain from the "violence of fist, tongue, or heart" *only* during demonstrations. No, they tasked volunteers to refrain from violence altogether. Even more: they subtly challenged volunteers, on the one hand, to think about violence in broad terms, to realize that physical violence is only one of myriad ways that we can be belligerent. On the other hand, organizers prodded volunteers to have a more expansive view of *nonviolence* as well: to understand that it was a physical, verbal, and spiritual exercise of peaceful power—one that required them to bring their whole selves to the table.

Our New Commitment

We must bring this understanding to our own practice of nonviolence, which is only as powerful as we are willing to make it or, more precisely, to *be* it.

One of the lessons that we can glean from the film footage of the campaign is that through nonviolence we actually come into power as well as express our own power. By this I mean that no matter how belligerent others may act toward us, we demonstrate that they cannot force us to engage them on their level and thus in the ways that they desire. The mobs who confronted the volunteers, for example, wanted their fear, their submission, *and* their retaliation. They got none of it. "They put us in jail," recalled Carlton Reese. "We were crowded together. We didn't have anywhere to sleep, but we weren't worried about sleeping. We carried on a lot of singing and praying in the jails. The guards and people in charge of all the prisoners would get highly upset, because when white people heard this kind of singing, it got to them. They really couldn't stand that kind of thing."[24]

By refusing, then, to satisfy another's craving for reciprocal violence and by offering instead to share the strength of our joy, compassion, and kindness, we model—as did the Birmingham volunteers—an alternative order and way of being that serve reconciliation and peace.

9. STRIVE to be in good spiritual and bodily health

Because volunteers were likely to face physical harm throughout the campaign, it was important to include this powerful commitment on the pledge card. The ninth encouraged volunteers to counter with practices of self-love the violence that they suffered. Indeed, the commitment implicitly construed self-care as a necessary means by which ordinary people would triumph over Birmingham's segregated order and achieve justice.

I take up this theme as a "new" commitment in chapter 4 (I focus specifically on the issue of bodily health). What the commitment suggests about the relationship between self-care and justice has particular salience for us today—especially given the myriad health challenges that many throughout our nation face, and most especially African American communities.

Suffice it to say that self-care is a pledge of nonviolence toward the self, an exercise of self-love the exclusion of which makes impossible our ability to live nonviolence completely. Therefore, in our journey, let us *seek and nurture good spiritual and bodily health practices for ourselves, for our families, and for society.*

10. FOLLOW **the directions of the movement and of the captain of a demonstration**

Though markedly different from the previous nine—it is not, like the others, especially aspirational—this final commitment is not entirely out of place. Here, organizers asked volunteers to maintain discipline, a challenge that implicitly underlies each and every one of the commitments.

In this regard, all ten commitments teach us that a life of nonviolence is ultimately the product of discipline and perseverance, a willingness to stick to a daily regimen of practices at which you sometimes fail and in which you sometimes lose faith—especially on days when you feel no one else is even remotely interested in living from a place of compassion, love, and peace. It requires work, in other words, and for this reason we take up the unspoken challenge of the Birmingham commitment card and simply pledge to *rededicate ourselves daily to nonviolence—for the freedom of all children, women, and men.*

Recite, then, these and the commitments that follow before you start your day. Read them on the bus, during lunch, or after dinner. Write them down and hang them on the wall in your office or carry them in your pocket so that you can read them whenever you are so moved. You could also attach them to your refrigerator door, where they will speak to you every time you reach for food. By doing these things, you'll make the commitments part of who you are and how you live your life.

A Promise for the Twenty-first Century

Practice forgiveness; extend compassion, love, and kindness to those who express and act with ill will; reestablish a connection to Earth; strive to be in good bodily health; cultivate hope—all of these commitments could very well have been included in the Birmingham pledge card. In fact, they were suggested to me by the "commandments" themselves and were articulated, in one way or another, throughout the course of the campaign and the civil rights movement generally.

In these "new" commitments I place front and center the legacies of slavery and Jim Crow and the work that these require of us on the path of nonviolence. As we near the end of Barack Obama's historic presidency, we are faced with an entirely different set of challenges that call into question the progress that many assumed his election in 2008 signified. As I write, the children, women, and men of Ferguson, Missouri, have taken to the streets to protest the death of Michael Brown, yet another young, unarmed African American man gunned down by the police. Like their Birmingham Campaign counterparts, the police of Ferguson have met the primarily peaceful protestors with police dogs in tow. Unlike their Birmingham counterparts, who had not been given military hardware from the Pentagon, the Ferguson police came fully armed with tanks and other firepower that we see deployed, simultaneously, in Gaza and Iraq—both of which are suffering unspeakable violence as a result.

Missouri's governor has called in the National Guard.

Ferguson's residents are under curfew.

Ferguson, Missouri, looks like a veritable war zone. Occupied territory.

Truly, such a moment calls for us to break open our hearts—to ground ourselves audaciously and unapologetically through practices of love—and to have heart, to speak out against and resist injustice, to insist on both reconciliation and freedom from state-sponsored violence, to speak truth to power, and *to be* peace. This is no less true for people of conscience today than it was for the children, women, and men of Birmingham who, fifty years ago, stood defiantly and nonviolently on the battle lines for freedom.

2 Practice Forgiveness

If we heal ourselves, we can heal our ancestors. We don't just practice for ourselves, we practice for all our ancestors.

—Thich Nhat Hanh[1]

First, we must develop and maintain the capacity to forgive. He who is devoid of the power to forgive is devoid of the power to love. It is impossible even to begin the act of loving one's enemies without the prior acceptance of the necessity, over and over again, of forgiving those who inflict evil and injury upon us.

—Martin Luther King Jr.[2]

Healing Our Ancestors

Although we might have an intuitive understanding of the role that practicing forgiveness plays in forging a life of nonviolence, the role that healing "our ancestors" plays might not be one that we intuitively grasp. Indeed, it might not be clear what healing "our ancestors" means or how it has anything at all to do with forgiveness, let alone nonviolence.

Nonetheless, as the teaching of the venerable Buddhist monk Thich Nhat Hanh implies, "healing our ancestors" is a practice integral to a life of nonviolence because it *is* a forgiveness practice. Through that practice, we come to terms not only with the harmful ways in which our ancestors—or the past more broadly—live in us and through us, but with the role that we play in perpetuating past harms and injustices. When we forgive our ancestors, we disarm our hearts and minds, reconcile and make peace with ourselves and others, and consequently learn to live in the world with a more forgiving and compassionate heart.

Hanh instructs us to undertake this forgiveness practice specifically by directing our attention to the harms or "negative seeds" that our near-ancestors, such as a deceased father or grandmother, might have passed on to us—either by inflicting harm directly or by modeling behaviors that we then take on as our own. "Maybe when you were young, you suffered so much already you are determined to be very different from your father," Hanh states. "You will never do what he has done to you. You were so determined, and yet because you don't know how to transform the energies that have been transmitted by him to you, when you grow up, you have the tendency to behave exactly like he did." According to Hanh, when we look honestly at ourselves and recognize that those "negative seeds" are in us and that, consequently, our ancestors continue to live *through* us (whether we like it or not), we can then practice "to diminish and to transform" the "negative seeds" that we've inherited. Just as critically, we can nurture "the positive seeds" that our ancestors passed on as well.

To diminish the "negative seeds," we can, for example, explore through meditation our negative "habit energies" or behaviors that derive from our ancestors, and become more mindful of them. We learn to notice, with a nonjudgmental and compassionate heart, when these habit energies (such as anger or ill will, for example) arise so we might release ourselves from them and the suffering that they cause us and others. Or we might manage to keep ourselves from getting caught by them in the first place.

Further, during our meditation we might choose to bring our specific ancestor (or ancestors) to mind and imagine her or him healed—free from the negativity from which she or he suffered and which caused so much suffering for those in her or his life.

We can also develop rituals through which we pay homage to our ancestors and bless them for the "positive seeds" that they passed on as well. "Every day I practice touching my ancestors," states Thich Nhat Hanh. "In my country, every home has an altar for ancestors. . . . Usually every morning we come and offer some incense to our ancestors. We want to light a stick of incense to our ancestors because the practice of lighting incense focuses our attention on the presence of our ancestors. During the time you strike the match [and] light the stick of incense . . . you have an opportunity to touch your ancestors within yourself. You realize that your ancestors are always alive in you because you are the continuation of your ancestors." We could incorporate in such a ritual as this practices that are steeped in our own heritage (in honor of my African heritage, for example, I might pour libations to my ancestors and call their names as I declare my forgiveness and intention to free us all).

Whatever particular practices we adopt, through them we move from a place of rejecting—that is, of banishing from our hearts—that father or grandmother to a place of acknowledging and accepting them and our connection to them. "We all have a family history that makes up a great part of who we are, whether we agree with what our ancestors did or not," writes Michele Benzamin-Miki. "[W]e suffer when we . . . disown a part of our history."[3] Through practice, we can begin to acknowledge and take care of our suffering. Just as importantly, we can begin to acknowledge our ancestors' suffering. This is a crucial step: for our embrace of nonviolence as a way of life presupposes our willingness to see that a person who does harm—and this most certainly includes us as well—suffers precisely because he is a person who has chosen to do harm. Such a person, we see, is in terrible need of a laying on of hands, whether he realizes it or not.

Because this practice is one we undertake with the full intention to heal the near-ancestor whom we believe caused us suffering, it is clearly a practice that requires us to open our hearts fully and to offer our forgiveness to that ancestor. But we also forgive ourselves. Indeed, we must forgive our *unforgiveness*, that is, forgive ourselves for the physical, emotional, and spiritual pain that we put ourselves through by closing off our hearts and/or cultivating ill will, as well as for harming others because we adopted the negative seeds of our forebears as our own.

The practice that Thich Nhat Hanh teaches is a wonderful way to honor our ancestors and release ourselves from "the pains of the past," as Jack Kornfield writes of forgiveness.[4] It is important to understand, however, that practicing forgiveness doesn't require us to believe that we literally heal our ancestors, or even to believe in their spiritual existence. The practice, first, enables us to come to terms with the ways in which we are held by the past as well as with how the past has shaped our lives. Secondly, it frees us to be more fully *in* the present moment because it helps us release our attachment to what no longer truly exists.

One of the great benefits of forgiveness is that it reveals to us just how much time, energy, and emotional as well as spiritual resources we used to keep alive within us experiences that had already come and gone. When we forgive, we discover we suddenly have more space in our minds and hearts for the present. Indeed, the "power of forgiveness," writes Michael Bernard Beckwith, "is liberating because it removes obstructions to the flow of good into our life."[5]

Thirdly, "healing our ancestors" helps us to accept the impermanence of all things—including the pains of the past. Because we release this pain, we realize it was never a permanent condition or feature of our lives. Finally, the practice allows us to see our ancestors as whole people who were always changing, shifting, becoming, and consequently were always more than the sum total of the harm they caused. When we see this, we can see ourselves more clearly as well.

Thus, healing our ancestors is of great benefit to us, to our progeny, and to our communities.

Nonetheless, I suggest that we go further, that we deepen and expand even more the practice of healing our ancestors. Although it is crucial to engage in a forgiveness practice that enables us to heal our past experiences with near-ancestors, we nevertheless remain in need of a healing that takes into account a broader notion of ancestry and allows us to come to terms, as well as reconcile our relationship with, our *historical past*—particularly our past in these United States. We must do more, in other words, than merely turn to and focus our forgiveness on a specific near-ancestor. We must also reach back and face the world in which they, as well as those before them, lived, with the understanding that we must begin to lay to rest—for our ancestors, ourselves, and our progeny—that world's pain and suffering.

Forgiveness Practice: Slavery and Jim Crow

When we practice to heal our ancestors, it is vital to include also as objects of our forgiveness the harms that were *visited upon* them. From African Americans' experience of being enslaved in as well as kidnapped and sold from Africa; to the agony of the Middle Passage and the despair of the auction block; to the lash of the overseer and the grief of watching a mother sold down the river; to the terror of the Klan and the indignities of having to drink from a water fountain labeled "Colored"—these harms require our healing attention, for what has surely been passed down from generation to generation is the pain of slavery and Jim Crow, the vestiges of which mark our everyday lives and a truth that for many of us causes suffering in the form of anger, shame, resentment, and ill will. Adding to our pain and suffering, of course, is the resistance on the part of many of our countrymen and -women to acknowledge these harms, to consider both reconciliation and reparations a just and ethical means to heal the present and the past, or even to deem our ancestors' pain worthy of their compassion and regard.

When we practice healing our ancestors in ways that include slavery and Jim Crow, we might do so by lovingly and compassionately holding our ancestors in our hearts as we call to mind the brutalities of these systems and the myriad ways in which they severely circumscribed as well as devalued the lives of our ancestors. To ensure that our practice is not abstract, we might call to mind a particular ancestor whose story of slavery, for example, survived—like the story of Mary Epps. Epps suffered the cruel and heart-wrenching experience—shared by many slaves—of watching helplessly while her owner sold many of her fifteen children. Upon the sale of one particular child, writes William Still, Mary "was so affected with grief" that "she was thrown into violent convulsions, which caused the loss of her speech for one entire month."[6]

Or there's the story of George, whose owner, writes Still, punished him by tying "both his wrists" with a rope and then hanging him in such a way that "George soon found himself hoisted on tip-toe with his feet almost clear of the floor." His owner's intent was to whip George in public. But when the crowd that gathered—"evidently" having "made up" its "mind that it would be more amusing to see the cowhiding than the circus"—was larger than George's owner expected, the latter was "seized with embarrassment" and decided not to carry out his punishment. Instead, he waited in "his office" for the crowd to disperse. During this time, however, George was left "hanging in mortal agony."[7]

Instead of reading a particular story, we might listen, for example, to Billie Holiday sing "Strange Fruit," and reflect on the state of terrorism under which many African Americans lived during the era of Jim Crow—a state that drove many African American families to migrate to the segregated cities of Northern states. Perhaps, while listening to the song, we'll specifically remember the fate of Emmett Till, the fourteen-year-old boy who, in 1955, was tortured and killed by a group of white men in Mississippi for allegedly flirting with a white woman.

Such stories bring home the meaning and measure of slavery and Jim Crow. What many of us might notice when we recall them is how much they stir up within us feelings of rage, despair, and ill will—to name only a few emotions. Not only does the violence that our ancestors suffered boggle the mind, but so also does the fact that people would treat others with such disregard: that they would establish systems, in fact, by which such treatment was rationalized and justified.

Let me suggest that our understandable moments of rage when we recall these stories and others are also, if not primarily, moments of pain. The pain stems from our inability to go back and protect our ancestors from violence; from our inability to change the past; and from the fact that systems are still in place that deny our humanity and thus continue to deny theirs. As such, these moments alert us, first of all, to the fact that we need to extend *to ourselves* a loving embrace and consciously sit still with the hurt that these stories evoke. By this I mean that we give ourselves permission to explore, perhaps through meditation, the hurt that is *in* the rage as well as to note the ways in which we might be holding that hurt in our bodies and in our collective consciousness.

As one who studied and taught African American literature, I have read many slave narratives as well as testaments to the cruelties of Jim Crow. Like most African Americans (I believe), I found such stories particularly painful to read, and so sometimes I could only read them in small doses. But instead of sitting with the pain itself, I frequently allowed myself to get swept up by rage and ill will. Or, I kept the pain and rage at bay through critical analysis, i.e., by examining "the texts" primarily in terms of the narrative devices employed by the authors.

Of course, there was nothing inherently wrong about my anger or about my use of critical analysis. Both can be powerful tools of transformation, if harnessed mindfully. For example, Audre Lorde wrote that anger when "expressed and translated into action in the service of our vision and future" is "a liberating and strengthening act of clarification."[8] Moreover, "not all anger is mindless or hate filled, and not all anger diminishes and destroys," writes Boesak. There would be "something deeply wrong" if we could "no longer be outraged by injustice and inhumanity."[9] Nevertheless, neither response actually put me in touch with the pain that I was feeling. In fact, both approaches enabled me to avoid it altogether, though the pain was certainly calling out for my attention.

When I recently revisited the slave narratives, I found myself once again enraged by what I was reading. This time around, however, instead of slamming my book down after a particularly difficult passage or expressing anger in other ways, I paused just long enough to keep myself from getting swept away. Just as importantly, I also paused long enough so I could take the time to feel fully, and even to begin to explore the depth, extent, and nature of the pain I had been holding about our historical past.

"When we are mindful of our feelings," writes Thich Nhat Hanh, "the situation begins to change. The feeling is no longer the only thing present in us, and it is transformed under the light of our awareness. Therefore, it no longer sweeps us along the way it did before there was mindfulness of the feeling. If we continue to observe the feeling mindfully, we will be able to see its substance and its roots. This kind of seeing empowers the observer."[10]

How much pain about slavery and Jim Crow, I wonder, might all of us be holding? How great is our need to lay hands on ourselves by—for example—sitting mindfully with that pain so that we might heal whatever hurt we might be feeling about our historical past?

The moments of rage alert us also to the fact that, though the past is long gone, we nevertheless are quite capable of making of it a living and breathing thing within that causes us to suffer. Much of that suffering, I imagine, can be traced to an unspoken wish for a better story, to our yearnings, perhaps, for a better past.

But the past cannot, and never will, be better. George will always be an ancestor who was left "hanging in mortal agony." Mary Epps will always be an ancestor whose children were sold. Their experiences are paradigmatic of the experiences of many of our ancestors (and are certainly not the worst of the worst), of which we can do nothing to assuage.

So where do we go from here? First of all, let us at least celebrate the fact that nothing is permanent. Slavery has been abolished in the United States, as has Jim Crow. Even Mary Epps and George made their way to freedom via the Underground Railroad. Things were and are not perfect, of course, and as Michelle Alexander argues so powerfully, a new form of Jim Crow has emerged in the guise of the "mass incarceration" of African Americans.[11] Thus, our work continues, but with our understanding that the impermanence of all things—which necessarily includes racism and white supremacy—is the truth of our existence.

Secondly, let us accept the fact that we "cannot make the past better." We do this because doing so is a powerful act of letting go and thus freeing ourselves from any pain we're carrying about our historical past. "The movement past blame," writes bell hooks, "can allow for a profound release of rage."[12] Through my experience of sitting with the pain that I felt when I read the slave narratives, for example, I was able to return to those narratives and read them without suffering so much rage. I approached them with this radically different intention: to forgive and to offer to our ancestors—as if they were sitting right beside me while I was reading their stories—a healing prayer. *May you be light in mind, body, and spirit. May you be safe and free from harm. May you be free from suffering.* I've done the same as well after looking at the detailed inventories that slave owners kept of their stock—my direct ancestors—including their purchase and sale prices.

Although my prayer did not change the past, it certainly changed *me*. Rage gave way to compassion; pain gave way to tenderheartedness; and a sense of powerlessness gave way to spiritual practice and a renewed commitment to creating a more just order.

From our acceptance of the fact that we cannot make the past better, we practice forgiveness. That is, as Kornfield says, we give up "all hope of a better past."[13] We accept that slavery and Jim Crow existed, and then we forgive that truth—forgive completely that these systems of violence constituted our ancestors' everyday lived experiences.

If it is true that forgiveness, as Martin Luther King Jr. argued, "is not an occasional act," but is instead "a permanent attitude," then, as tempting as it might be, we cannot possibly leave slavery and Jim Crow off of the table.[14] We cultivate a permanent attitude of forgiveness precisely by ferreting out unforgiveness wherever it resides in our hearts, minds, and spirits.

Yet, this is also true: while we "recall the terrible past so that we can deal with it, forgiving where forgiveness is necessary," as Nelson Mandela advised at the end of his service as president of South Africa, we must "never" forget.[15] Indeed, "our duty," as Elie Wiesel so eloquently states about the Holocaust, "is to bear witness for the dead *and* the living. [We have] no right to deprive future generations of a past that belongs to our collective memory. To forget would not only be dangerous but offensive."[16]

Indeed, it would be dangerous to forget, especially when we consider how determined some people are to turn back the clock on the rights that our ancestors and elders fought so hard to secure. It is not for nothing that many communities in the South and beyond have acted quickly to adopt restrictive voting policies once the U.S. Supreme Court, in its 2013 decision *Shelby v. Holder*, effectively gutted the Voting Rights Act.

We, therefore, forgive *and* we remember, and we remember by refusing to internalize and cooperate with the violent and spirit-killing legacies of slavery and Jim Crow, as well as the myriad ways that they manifest in our daily lives. Our ancestors, I believe, would have wished for us such healing and activism, and so this work that we do for ourselves is one that fulfills their hopes that their progeny would lead lives of peace and freedom from suffering.

To extend such forgiveness is no small matter, and it should not be undertaken with anything less than our full commitment. Whereas we might, as Howard Thurman argued, "very glibly . . . use such words as 'sympathy,' 'compassion'" and (I would add) "forgiveness," in "experience it is genuinely to be rocked to one's foundations."[17] To forgive something as treacherous as slavery and Jim Crow can only be a truly life-changing experience. One will not come out of this practice the same person that went in.

Forgiveness Practice: Our Ancestors' Suffering

> *The black experience in America . . . begins with suffering. It begins in the violence of seventeenth-century slave forts sprinkled along the west coast of Africa, where debtors, thieves, war prisoners, and those who would not convert to Islam were separated from their families, branded, and sold to Europeans who packed them into pestilential ships that cargoed 20 million human beings (a conservative estimate) to the New World. Only 20 percent of those slaves survived the harrowing voyage at sea (and only 20 percent of the sailors, too), and if they were among the lucky few to set foot on American soil, new horrors and heartbreak awaited them.*
>
> —**Charles Johnson**[18]

We can go even deeper with our practice. Having come to some measure of peace regarding the systems of slavery and Jim Crow, we heal our ancestors further by forgiving the fact that they suffered.

To be sure, in spite of the brutalities of slavery and Jim Crow, African Americans lived lives of great beauty, grace, dignity, and joy, to which we have borne and continue to bear witness through our literature and music, histories and art, politics and spiritual journeying. To bear witness in these ways is itself a healing practice, for we rescue from the tragedies of history their triumphs and dogged perseverance to claim their humanity despite all efforts to dehumanize them. Nonetheless, there is still that unspeakable suffering that calls for healing and makes elusive reconciliation, if not in this nation, then most certainly within our own bodies and spirits.

To put this in perspective, consider these questions: How might the trauma that was endured by a great-great-great-grandmother when a slave owner branded her with a hot iron, for example, continue to be living and breathing in her great-great-great-grandson? And how might he come to recognize that trauma's residence *in* him, so he might heal himself and all of his grandmothers?

When we practice healing our ancestors by including the physical, emotional, and spiritual pain that they suffered, we can meditate on such questions as these—and not so much come up with definitive answers (though if we can, that's certainly a good thing), but instead bear witness to pain that, more likely than not, we are unable to trace directly but that nevertheless burns a path from the past to the present. Maybe it has shown up in gestures or in an inflection. Maybe it is in the color of our skin or in the walls of our arteries. Or maybe it announces itself in the way that we discipline our children (or don't). Perhaps it is rage or despair or hopelessness or fear or mental illness or submission to "the way things are," all of which gets explained as merely the peculiar character of the family or community.

Whatever the case, to heal our ancestors, and thus to heal ourselves, we turn and bear witness to their suffering, forgiving it all. And then we seal this healing by refusing to claim violence as our own. Just as we might refuse to spank our children because of the "whuppin'" we suffered at the hands of our parents, we might choose to repudiate violence in thought, word, and deed—to leave it in the past as a dead thing unworthy of resurrection through us—because of the suffering that it created in the past and the suffering that it creates for us today, for our nation as a whole.

Or how about this? We could seal this healing by embracing the idea that we actually *deserve* nonviolence, both as a state of being and as the basis of our interactions with and treatment by others.

Forgiveness Practice: Including Our White Ancestors

There is still more that we can do to heal our ancestors. Our practice, if it is to be complete, must also include our white ancestors, and most especially those who perpetrated the harms of slavery and Jim Crow.

This practice we undertake by first grounding ourselves in an observation about hate that Martin Luther King Jr. offered to his parishioners during the heyday of the civil rights movement. "Another reason why we must love our enemies," King wrote, "is that hate scars the soul and distorts the personality. Mindful that hate is an evil and dangerous force, we too often think of what it does to the person hated. This is understandable, for hate brings irreparable damage to its victims. . . . But there is another side that we must never overlook. Hate is just as injurious to the person who hates."

Like "an unchecked cancer," King explained further, hate also "corrodes" and "eats" the "vital unity" of the perpetrator's personality. Moreover, not only does it destroy the perpetrator's "sense of values" and "objectivity"; hate also distorts the perpetrator's sense of reality, for it "causes him to describe the beautiful as ugly and the ugly as beautiful, and to confuse the true with the false and the false with the true."[19] For these reasons, the person who hates is a victim of the very "force" by which he or she seeks to harm others.

Whereas King's focus on the suffering of "the person who hates" constituted an effort on his part to cut through any resistance among movement participants to see their "enemies" as people in need of the healing power of forgiveness and love, it was also a means by which he sought to undercut the unspoken presumption that systems of subordination like Jim Crow and their "injurious" effects were neutral with regard to perpetrators of injustice. For King, this presumption was not only spiritually untenable, it was also politically untenable in that it signified a failure to frame justice in broader terms. King believed that such a failure made elusive the realization of "Beloved Community." He, therefore, invited those who were committed to justice to pay attention to "the oppressors'" peculiar suffering.

Admittedly, the very idea that perpetrating injustice constitutes suffering in action is not one most people embrace or even believe. If anything, we tend to view the infliction of harm as part and parcel of the lived experience—and, by extension, *the pleasurable benefit*—of privilege. It is impossible to be blind, for example, to the joy on the faces of a lynch mob that proudly posed for photographs near the black man it subsequently burned at the stake; or the glee with which the police who confronted the Birmingham demonstrators released their dogs;

or, more currently, the pleasure with which some talking heads and radio-show hosts promote racism, sexism, and homophobia.

Nonetheless, if we pause for a moment to consider our own hateful acts, thoughts, and speech, we cannot help but see our suffering in them. If there is pleasure, then it is most certainly twisted; if there is joy, underneath is despair. For anyone who has experienced *schadenfreude*, there is something fundamentally painful about offering hate to, and cutting oneself off from, others, even if one's stated reasons for doing so are self-preservation and self-respect.

It is not hard to see, if we look deeply, the costs of hate to those who perpetuate it. The lack of humanity that it reveals, not to mention the fear, should be evidence enough of the suffering involved. More to the point: To be so out of touch with love, compassion, and grace as to take pleasure in and benefit from another's pain and despair speaks volumes to an unspeakable level of suffering, for which we should all have great compassion.

In fact, "peace, and a willingness to be patient in the face of such enormous provocation and suffering," writes Jon Kabat-Zinn, "can only come about through the inner cultivation of compassion, a compassion that is not limited to friends, but is felt equally for those who, out of ignorance and often seen as evil, may cause you and those you love to suffer."[20]

So we turn to our white ancestors, many of whom held and sold their own children as property (Founding Father Thomas Jefferson immediately comes to mind), and practice to heal them as well. We do this because it is our charge, as Howard Thurman writes, to "make again and again an act of faith toward" all men and women, including those who have thrived on the suffering of others. "If this is not done," Howard cautions, "any discussion even of love is an empty echo among the barren hills of a desolate experience."[21]

Thus, we forgive the fact that our white ancestors harmed their black brothers and sisters, harmed themselves as a result, and in so doing created a legacy of suffering for future generations. To these ancestors, we whisper as well a prayer: *May you be light in mind, body, and spirit. May you be safe and free from harm. May you and your progeny be free from the suffering of hatred, of racism, and of enmity.*

Forgiveness, History, and the Birmingham Campaign

To include our historical past as an object of our forgiveness is actually not too far removed from the spirit of the original Birmingham Campaign commitment card. Indeed, even though you won't find the word *forgiveness* anywhere on the card itself, the card implicitly prescribes as necessary to a life of nonviolence practicing forgiveness, and practicing in ways that include our historical past.

To see this, it is important to recognize that, in asking volunteers for their promise to seek, for example, "justice and reconciliation," or to "walk and talk in the manner of love"—and to do so *in spite of the hate and violence that they faced*—campaign organizers were really asking them to practice forgiveness. After all, how can one seek reconciliation or walk and talk in the manner of love and yet be unforgiving at the same time? Indeed, the organizers were asking volunteers to practice a forgiveness so profound that they would be able to offer their "enemies" their "brotherly" love. This was by far the most difficult challenge that they asked the volunteers to meet (and, frankly, loving one's "enemies" is the most difficult challenge for anyone who seeks to live a life of nonviolence).

That the volunteers would have had to lay down the burden of any ill will concerning the past in order to offer such love is clear. For in order to embrace one's "enemies" as "brothers," one has to move through and forgive the past deeds that created enmity in the first instance. The challenge was not that the volunteers were to forget the past; instead, the challenge was that they were to honor it by repairing the present through the power of forgiveness and love—as expressed, of course, by nonviolent, passive resistance.

I don't know whether or not, or to what degree, the volunteers were able to meet the challenge. But I do know that meeting it is work that nonviolence requires of us. By pledging our willingness to forgive, and to include within our forgiveness our historical past, we create possibilities for reconciliation in all facets of our lives.

We also, I might add, heal and liberate all of our ancestors.

3 Extend Compassion, Love, and Kindness to Those Who Express and Act with Ill Will

We have not come into this exquisite world
To hold ourselves hostage from love.

—**Hafiz**[1]

Enemies

Since this nation elected its first African American president in 2008, hate speech–tainted conversations concerning issues of national importance—health care, immigration, unemployment, national security, to give a few examples—have increasingly permeated and infected the public sphere. It is virtually impossible these days to scan the Internet, read or watch the news, listen to the radio, peruse Facebook, watch C-SPAN, or simply walk down the street without encountering and being assaulted by somebody's hatred.

Those of us who are regular targets of hate speech have every reason to conclude that we are under siege, surrounded by "enemies" who are increasingly emboldened to express their desire to visit upon us tremendous harm—whether in the form of public policies designed to secure our subordination or outright violence. Many of you might remember, for example, former North Carolina GOP Precinct Chair Don Yelton's advocacy for a voter ID law that will, without a doubt, have a negative impact on the voting rights of African Americans and poor people in his state. Yelton reasoned that if the law "hurts the whites so be it. If it hurts a bunch of lazy blacks that want the government to give them everything, so be it."[2] Or perhaps you recall the murder of Mark Carson, who was shot in the face while walking in Greenwich Village. Moments before the killing, murder suspect Elliot Morales taunted Carson with the slurs "queer" and "faggot."[3] Incidents such as these—of which there are, sadly, far too many to name—put to the test probably the most difficult challenge one faces as one traverses the path of nonviolence: to "love your enemies."

As was the case fifty years ago for the Birmingham Campaign volunteers, we are presented with the choice of responding to incredible hostility either with love or with hate. That is, we must decide—as the Birmingham volunteers had to decide—just how deeply committed we are to the principles of nonviolence.

The Practice of Love

> *Love is a practice and unless you know what suffering is, you are not motivated to practice compassion, love, and understanding.*
>
> **—Thich Nhat Hanh**[4]

Although the prescription to "love your enemies" is not a commandment that was included on the Birmingham Campaign commitment card, it was nevertheless the ultimate commitment that the volunteers were asked to make. After all, love is the ground upon which nonviolence rests, and it is to love that we surrender when we choose to live a life of nonviolence. As Martin Luther King Jr. put it, "at the center of nonviolence stands the principle of love."[5]

"Love your enemies" is implied in many, if not most, of the campaign card commitments. For example, "PRAY daily to be used by God in order that all men might be free" and "SACRIFICE personal wishes in order that all men might be free" subtly challenged volunteers, through the words "all men," to include their adversaries within their vision of Beloved Community. In other words, these commitments charged volunteers to pray and sacrifice personal wishes in order to secure freedom not merely for some, but for all. To do this, volunteers would need to open their hearts to and embrace their "enemies" as brothers and sisters, and to see them also in need of liberation.

The commitment to "WALK and TALK in the manner of love, for God is love" also conveys the message to "love your enemies," in the sense that it challenged volunteers to demonstrate in all aspects of their lives an all-inclusive (godlike) love, i.e., to love without discrimination as to who is worthy and who is unworthy, who is friend and who is foe.

You might be wondering why campaign organizers didn't just list "love your enemies" on the commitment card, especially considering how crucial this idea is to the philosophy of nonviolence. What was the point of subsuming it *within* the commitments instead of stating it outright?

The answer lies, I believe, in the commitments' emphasis on *acts,* an emphasis that seems to suggest that organizers excluded the express directive to "love your enemies" precisely because the ability to offer such love hinges on whether or not one actually *practices*, at the level of everyday life, an all-inclusive love. In other words, the organizers knew—as we no doubt understand intuitively—that the capacity to love your "enemies" isn't something that happens magically or simply because you've been encouraged to do so. You can only rise to this difficult challenge by cultivating habits and skills (for example, praying and sacrificing personal wishes as well as walking and talking in the manner of love) that will enable you to break down and break through whatever barriers you have erected to keep you from seeing what enmity actually reveals. What it reveals is not only that those who hate suffer because of their hatred (as discussed in the previous chapter), but they are ultimately driven, as Howard Thurman has argued, by an unspoken and unmet need to feel as if their joy and well-being matter to others. Behind all of their "hostility, hate, and antisocial behavior," theorizes Thurman, "the hunger persists—the ache to be cared for," and for themselves "alone."[6]

In other words, they're human.

When you practice love on a day-to-day basis, you open yourself up in ways that enable you to realize at the level of the heart the wisdom of the observation that—as *A Course in Miracles* puts it—"every loving thought is true; everything else is an appeal for healing and help, regardless of the form it takes."[7] In other words, you see clearly that enmity itself is someone's appeal for healing, help, and, I would add, compassion. This knowledge should awaken within you a generosity of spirit, a desire to exercise *radical care* by answering with love your "enemies'" plea—even if that plea is expressed in terrible ways.

Without cultivating some kind of daily practice, however, without doing the work that will ultimately enable us to notice and have compassion for our "enemies," the ability to love them is simply not possible. In such a situation, "love" itself remains a mere aspiration that can easily give way—in the face of hostility—to bitterness, hatred, retaliation, and even violence. This is what the Birmingham Campaign organizers knew, and why they directed the volunteers' energy and attention to practices of love.

So, develop daily practices of love that speak to you and then pursue them with abandon. You could, for instance, do something as simple as help a mother lift a baby carriage onto a bus. Or perhaps you'll make a commitment to wish everyone you encounter (including the "difficult" people you know) a beautiful day. Maybe you'll relinquish your seat on the subway to someone who seems tired and stressed. You can practice love in countless ways, which may prove to be perfectly disarming for those on the receiving end. Such practice might help them to let go of whatever tension or hurt they might be carrying. A kind greeting from a stranger, for example, often is enough to shift my consciousness from stress and worry to lightness. It reminds me that I can return such a gift to others.

Whatever you choose to do, stick with your practices and be guided by your intention to cultivate a heart big enough to include and to respond compassionately to the call of those who wish you harm. Though you will certainly falter, remember that love is perfected with practice.

A Relationship Between Equals

Before we even begin to meet the challenge of answering our "enemies'" appeal, we must first answer our own. In other words, we have to face our own investment in dislike or enmity toward others. As Pema Chödrön instructs, "compassion is not a relationship between the healer and the wounded." Instead, it is "a relationship between equals. Only when we know our own darkness well can we be present with the darkness of others. Compassion becomes real when we recognize our shared humanity."[8]

Thus, you might want to take a moment to examine whether or not there is someone in your life whom you regard with intense dislike, anger, ill will, or hate. When you visualize that person, what thoughts come to mind? Do you imagine yourself speaking to her or him with rage or disrespect? Do you see yourself cutting that person down with your words, or perhaps even physically? Is your imagined confrontation one in which you emerge the vanquisher? Do you keep feeding your anger with new battles and new triumphs?

If you find yourself going down that road, check in to see how your journeying makes you feel. Does your body become just as engulfed with ill will as your mind? For example, do you tense up, send your stomach into turmoil, clench your teeth, or become more aggressive or physical?

Does any of this make you feel joyful and at peace? If your response is that it makes you feel "good" to play out these scenarios, then is that "good" the same "good" that you feel when you bring to mind someone whom you love and cherish? And when you are finished, when you have exhausted yourself or have chased an entirely different thought altogether, are you the better for having harbored and fed your ill will and hate? Has it made you a more loving, kind, thoughtful, and *just* person?

When we start to dissect our own ill will, we can begin to acknowledge that it actually causes *us* to suffer—physically, emotionally, and spiritually. This is poignantly illustrated by the story of Elwin Wilson, a former member of the Ku Klux Klan who brutally beat Georgia Congressman John Lewis in 1961 when the latter disembarked at the Rock Hill, South Carolina, Greyhound bus terminal. Lewis was one of the Freedom Riders organized by the Congress of Racial Equality to challenge segregation on interstate buses and bus facilities. In 2009, a few months after the nation elected President Obama, Wilson called on Lewis to apologize for beating him and harming others in the heyday of the civil rights movement. "All I can say is that it has bothered me for years, all the bad stuff I've done," Wilson said. "And I found out there is no way I could be saved and get to heaven and still not like blacks." According to Wilson's wife, Wilson had carried "on his heart for a long time" the Lewis beating and other acts of racist violence on his part. He wished,

Wilson's wife stated, that "he could find the ones he mistreated and apologize to them all."[9]

Anyone who witnessed Wilson's apology to Lewis could see just how deeply Wilson suffered from his hate and violence. As Lewis put it, "Elwin Wilson experienced what Martin Luther King Jr. told all of us[:] that 'hate is too heavy a burden to bear.'"[10] More pointedly, what Wilson experienced demonstrated that "hatred, which could destroy so much, never failed to destroy the man who hated," as James Baldwin writes.[11]

Wilson's lead, I believe, is a good one to follow. Like him, we can face our ill will and the ways it has made us suffer. (Who knows just how much of Wilson's hate contributed to the heart problems he suffered later in his life?) We can allow this truth to break our hearts wide open—wide enough for us to see how, by cultivating ill will, we have alienated ourselves from our own physical, emotional, and spiritual good, and from our unspoken and unmet need to be cared for and regarded. "I imagine one of the reasons people cling to their hates so stubbornly," Baldwin suggests, "is because they sense, once hate is gone, they will be forced to deal with pain."[12] Facing the pain of disregard, we will in the process realize that our need for care would never *and could never* have been satisfied by our hate, for to hate is to invite ill will and hate in return. Moreover, it is simply true that cultivating ill will toward others spills over into, and colors, other areas of our lives. It feeds an attitude of negativity and prepares a way for us to see all people through the prism of our hostility.

Like Wilson, then, we must let go of our animosity with

the confidence of knowing that, in the end, it never really served us. To those whom we have harmed with our dislike or hateful thoughts, words, or deeds, we can, again like Wilson, offer to them our apology. Or, at the very least, we can extend to them our wish that they will always be the recipients of love, care, and goodwill. The challenge "to love your enemies," after all, is not only a challenge to love those who wish you harm; it is also a challenge *to transform your own enmity* and to become the reconciliation that you seek in the world. This, too, is what Elwin Wilson showed us, as Congressman Lewis writes. Wilson demonstrated "that people can change, and when they put down the mechanisms of division and separation to pick up the tools of reconciliation, they can help build a greater sense of community in our society, even between the most unlikely people. Elwin Wilson proves that we are all one people, one family, the human family, and what affects one of us affect [*sic*] us all."[13]

Honoring the Gate of Suffering

> *When we honor the gate of suffering, what arises is the wondrous power of compassion.*
>
> —**Jack Kornfield**[14]

Having transformed our own enmity, we can turn authentically toward those who direct ill will our way and answer their appeal for help, healing, and compassion.

Who in your everyday life—acquaintances, family members, coworkers, neighbors—has made you the object of her ill will? Or, who in the public sphere has disparaged the group with which you identify and are identified? For just a moment, bring this person to mind and reflect on all the various ways in which she or he expresses ill will—the way she or he talks, her or his facial expressions, body language, tone of voice. Don't judge what you see; simply observe and take note.

I practice this often when I watch on television talking heads present—usually with undisguised contempt and venom toward a broad swath of the population—their take on the political, social, and economic issues of the day. I usually start off enraged by their "analysis" (which is, of course, precisely the emotional response that many of them apparently hope to elicit). If I can manage to collect myself—an admittedly difficult feat, especially after I have already launched into my own furious "rebuttal"—I'll take a deep breath so that I can quietly watch and listen. Eventually, I start to focus my attention less on what they say and more on *how* they communicate.

What happens next is always an unsettling, if not eye-opening experience. In their gestures, expressions, and tone, *I actually see myself.* That is, I see what I look like and hear what I sound like when I have acted and spoken with unkindness or ill intent. Moreover, I recognize that my initial response to these talking heads was itself a mirror image of the ill will with which they are consumed.

However, an even more crucial insight takes hold: because I see me, *I can also see their suffering*. That is, I recognize the suffering *in* their ill will—the signs of the physical, emotional, and spiritual toll that their ill will takes—because it is suffering that I have known for myself, even though it was partially masked (as it is for them) by expressions of self-satisfaction, if not downright self-righteousness.

Trust me when I say that this experience pierces whatever armor you might be using to protect yourself from connecting with your "enemies." By relating to them through your own experience of suffering, you create an opening through which compassion can enter your heart and move you to a higher place. It is a place from which you can see not only that your "enemies" are in tremendous need of care, but also that you are absolutely capable of giving it. Indeed, you see that just as you can extend your compassion, love, and kindness to heal the "negative seeds" planted by your ancestors (as discussed in the preceding chapter), you can do the same for those who, in the present moment, nurture "negative seeds" by directing toward you their ill will or hatred.

So adopt for yourself practices (like watching talking heads, for example) through which you intentionally open yourself up to the humanity of those who wish you harm. You might start off by grounding yourself in the truth that Bob Marley wanted us always to remember: "the biggest man you ever did see was once a baby."[15] These words remind us not only that those who wish us harm are not actually larger than life, but that no one, as Nelson Mandela observed, "is born hating another person because of the color of his skin, or his background, or his religion. People must learn to hate, and if they can learn to hate, they can be taught to love, for love comes more naturally to the human heart than its opposite."[16]

Through practices in which we surrender to love, we come to the understanding—even if only for a moment—that we truly have no "enemies." Instead, we see that we are surrounded by brothers and sisters who are suffering in one form or another, but who are expressing it as hatred. This being the case, shouldn't we just drop the word "enemies" altogether?

No doubt you have noticed by now that I have been placing quote marks around the word *enemies*, and the reason is this: to claim that we have "enemies" whom we must learn to love is to embrace in some measure the idea of a foe. It is to internalize the violence inherent in enmity, and thus to perpetuate—albeit inadvertently—the self/other framework that has fueled so much violence in the world. Indeed, to use the term "enemies" might even make it more difficult for us to imagine the person who harbors ill will and perpetrates injustice as one who suffers and is in need of our compassion, love, and kindness. Thus, as part of our embrace of nonviolence, it is best we drop the term altogether, even though the command to "love your enemies" has been, for quite some time, a staple of the discourse on nonviolence.

Turning to our brothers and sisters, we can—as we did with our ancestors—offer our forgiveness. We forgive them for their enmity, and we do so with the clarity that comes from knowing that all of us are profoundly injured by any ill will or hate that we harbor and express, and are thus all in need of forgiveness. With love in our hearts, we also offer to them an invitation to join us in creating Beloved Community, and we do so because their citizenship is both necessary and desired.

Such was the marvelous example set by Congressman John Lewis, whose response to Elwin Wilson not only "demonstrated the power of love"—to use the words with which Lewis described Wilson; it also revealed to the world just how powerful is the willingness to answer another's call for healing, help, and compassion. Without any hesitation whatsoever, Lewis responded to Wilson's evident suffering by shaking Wilson's hand, embracing him, and then offering Wilson the medicine that he seemed to need most: "I forgive you. I don't have any bitterness or hatred."[17]

One can only imagine how healing those words were for Wilson—and how healing it was for Lewis to say them.

We all "make blunders," John Lewis stated years later, after learning of the former Klansman's death. But as nonviolence teaches, each one of us can "get on the right road toward building a greater sense of community."[18]

Love Is Not Like

If the idea of loving "your enemies" is still challenging for you, perhaps it would ease your mind to know that love does not mean "like," as Martin Luther King Jr. explained. "We should be happy that [Jesus] did not say, 'Like your enemies.' It is almost impossible to like some people. 'Like' is a sentimental and affectionate word. How can we be affectionate and sentimental toward a person whose avowed aim is to crush your very being and place innumerable stumbling blocks in your path? How can we like a person who is threatening our children and bombing our homes? That is impossible."[19]

I confess that during those moments when I was able to connect with the talking heads through the suffering that I know enmity creates for me, I did not, as a result, find myself *liking* them. No, I did not like them at all. And I suspect that I would find it impossible to like them under any circumstances.

But love—that is a feeling I was able both to generate and sustain, at least for some time. Let me be clear: when I speak of "love," I mean "an attitude of wanting to help other sentient beings enjoy happiness"—which is "love" as it is defined from a Buddhist perspective.[20] Since "you know what suffering is," writes Thich Nhat Hanh, then you "don't want to make other people suffer, and therefore your love is born. You want to be happy and you want to bring happiness to others. That is love."[21]

To love in this way is not to get caught up in or stuck on your likes and dislikes about others. Instead, it is to care radically for others, to see their well-being and yours as inextricably bound. This includes the well-being of those who genuinely wish you harm. In fact, since you see the latter more clearly after you have abandoned your reactiveness to their enmity, you are just as motivated to end their suffering as you are "to work" generally "for the benefit of others," as the Dalai Lama puts it.[22]

Does embodying this kind of love mean that we surrender our critical discernment as well as resistance to the hateful thoughts and deeds of others? Not by any stretch of the imagination. Instead, we simply understand that we all, to varying degrees, walk in the world feeling vulnerable about life, meaning, friendship, and regard. In spite of our differences, all of us are doing our best to sort out and make sense of this seemingly incomprehensible project we call "life." In this way, we are absolutely connected and have the capacity to bring happiness to one another and thereby to alleviate one another's suffering.

The Radicalism of Our Time

Compassion is the radicalism of our time.

—Dalai Lama XIV[23]

Ultimately, to care radically boils down to our answering affirmatively the question: Are we willing to embrace fully the work of loving one another *into being* Beloved Community? To do so is what a life committed to nonviolence requires, for it is through such work that we create the conditions that enable all of us to relinquish ill will, hate, and violence. "Nonviolence," Howard Thurman writes, "is one of the great vehicles of reconciliation because it creates and maintains a climate in which the need to be cared for and understood can be honored and effectively dealt with. . . . It presupposes that the desire to be cared for and to care for others is one with the very essence of all one's meaning and significance."[24]

Thus, we offer to those who wish us harm the blessing suggested by Joseph Goldstein: "May you be free of hatred, may you be free of enmity." After all, "if our aspiration is peace in the world," then can there really be anyone "we would exclude from this wish"? Hatred and enmity "are the mind states that drive harmful acts," and if "our own response is enmity or hatred or ill will, whether we acknowledge it or not, we are part of the problem."[25]

But we don't stop there. To care radically also means that we must work to dismantle the political, economic, and social structures from which those who wish us harm "benefit." After all, you cannot care for them (or yourself, for that matter) and yet leave intact the systems through which they reify, express, and impose their ill will, i.e., their suffering.

Indeed, this is a crucial lesson of the Birmingham Campaign and the civil rights movement in general. By casting Birmingham's white community as a community *injured* by the system of segregation—and injured *in spite of* the fact that it reaped political, economic, and social rewards from this system—the organizers of the campaign were able to frame the struggle as a broader effort to free the *entire* Birmingham community from the suffering that was segregation. As Martin Luther King Jr. put it, the nonviolent movement enabled "the Negro . . . to transmute hatred into constructive energy, to seek not only to free himself but to free his oppressor from his sins. This transformation, in turn, had the marvelous effect of changing the face of the enemy. The enemy the Negro faced became not the individual who had oppressed him but the evil system which permitted that individual to do so."[26] It mattered little, therefore, that many whites enjoyed and thus fought to maintain their privileges. Their enjoyment simply signified just how thoroughly harmed they were by, and how deeply they suffered under, the system of segregation. Thus, by working to dismantle segregation, movement participants were, in effect, exercising nothing less than compassionate and radical care, bringing on a healing that was necessary to ensure the well-being and authentic happiness of white and black citizens alike.

What this result suggests is that any failure on our part to love those who harbor and express ill will toward us and to consider their peculiar suffering renders incomplete our conception of rights and our strategies for the achievement of justice. If we seek freedom for *all* children, women, and men, we must want the perpetrators of injustice to be free from suffering. This is what makes compassion both radical and a vow of "nonviolence to everything."[27]

As we commit to dismantling the structures from which those who hate "benefit," we must with great intention replace them with systems that, in John Lewis's words, heal "the wounded souls in our society, the soul of the victim as well as the perpetrator." Such action will require our persistent and explicit naming of the privileges, benefits, and advantages that have been and continue to be purchased at the expense of others as in fact harms experienced by those in power.

Love Is Not Special

> *Hate is a dead thing. Who of you would be a tomb?*
>
> **—Khalil Gibran**[28]

It may go without saying that those who hate will likely reject outright our overtures and will probably resist the idea that their privileges, benefits, and advantages constitute harm and suffering. This, too, is a lesson of the Birmingham Campaign and the civil rights movement. Though campaign and movement participants expressed their desire for reconciliation and healing for all from the harm that was racial segregation, their aspirations were answered more with fire hoses, police dogs, angry mobs, bombs, and other forms of violence than they were with peace, love, and care. Since the movement, efforts to address privilege at all levels of society have met with stiff resistance. So, there's no need to expect our efforts to be embraced with open arms.

Martin Luther King Jr. spoke often of such resistance when he advocated for nonviolence. "I do not want to give the impression that nonviolence will work miracles overnight," he wrote. "Men are not easily moved from their mental ruts or purged of their prejudiced and irrational feelings. When the underprivileged demand freedom, the privileged first react with bitterness and resistance. Even when the demands are couched in nonviolent terms, the initial response is the same. . . . So the nonviolent approach does not immediately change the heart of the oppressor."[29]

But in the end, that's quite all right, because nonviolence "does something to the hearts and souls of those committed to it." Not only does it give "them new self-respect," as King argues; it also "calls up resources of strength and courage that they did not know they had."[30]

In fact, when we pivot toward our hate-consumed brothers and sisters from an ethic of nonviolence and thus from our intention to love, we come into our own inherent power. In truth, our love is itself an act of disobedience toward, or noncooperation with, the status quo of hate, whether expressed through institutions or by individuals whom we encounter. It is our promise that we intend to manifest a different order altogether, one that reflects the wisdom that comes from understanding that "love is not special"[31]—that it is, instead, something to extend joyfully to all without exception. As Howard Thurman wrote, "love has no awareness of merit or demerit; it has no scale by which its portion may be weighed or measured. It does not seek to balance giving and receiving. Love loves; this is its nature."[32]

So we love, confident that the Elwin Wilsons of the world will eventually come around, confident that the just systems that we create will heal the ones that don't. By practicing love—as the Birmingham Campaign volunteers were encouraged to do—we will have made it possible to see our "enemies" as our brothers and sisters whom we will welcome, with the same spirit that John Lewis welcomed Elwin Wilson, to the grand project of "building a greater sense of community."[33]

4 Reestablish a Connection to Earth

In a real sense, all life is interrelated. All men are caught in an inescapable network of mutuality, tied in a single garment of destiny. Whatever affects one directly affects all indirectly. I can never be what I ought to be until you are what you ought to be, and you can never be what you ought to be until I am what I ought to be. This is the interrelated structure of reality.

—Martin Luther King Jr.[1]

We are a people who have always loved life and loved the earth. We have noticed Earth. How responsive and alive it is. We have appreciated it. We have been a nation of creators and farmers who adored the Earth even when we were not permitted to own any part of it larger than our graves. And then only until a highway needed to be built or a condominium constructed on top of them.

—Alice Walker[2]

All Life Is Interrelated

When we embrace nonviolence as a way of life, we project—as Martin Luther King Jr. instructed—"the ethic of love" or *agape* "to the center of our lives."[3] That is to say, we embody as well as demonstrate through our words and by our deeds the idea that "all life is interrelated." Though we live in a society that places a great (and ultimately costly) premium on rugged, possessive individualism and on the autonomous self, the fact is that whatever we do *individually* affects the lives of others, even if only in some small way. Realizing this, we make a commitment to ourselves and to everyone to do no harm. Yet we also make a commitment to do justice, to "meet the needs" of our sisters and brothers, *to be* peace. For if it is true that "whatever affects one directly affects all indirectly," then we might as well "affect all" with as much joy, care, and grace as we can possibly bear.

Of course, we ourselves do not escape the effects of our words or actions. To the contrary, we are directly and indirectly affected by all of what we say or do to others. Thus, "to the degree that I harm my brother, no matter what he is doing to me," King wrote, "to that extent I am harming myself."[4] Or as the Buddha framed it, "if we truly loved ourselves, we would not harm another."[5] What is also true, of course, is that to the degree that we *care* for our sister, to that extent we care for ourselves.

All of this makes intuitive sense. If you reflect on a time when you were generous with your resources, or listened to a friend in need, or helped a stranger with directions, you would probably recall that such givingness on your part blessed you with a sense of fullness and well-being. Perhaps the rest of your day was joyful as a result; perhaps you continued to extend kindness to others, thereby multiplying your happiness. Such experiences are unassailable evidence of the goodness that returns to us when we are good to others.

It is, therefore, a tremendous demonstration of self-love and self-care to offer to others, for example, our generosity, kindness, presence, and respect. And when we live in this way, we invite others to demonstrate their own self-regard—an act that truly expresses the essence of nonviolence. By projecting the ethic of love to the center of our lives, then, we bring out the best in all of us. Even if, however, those to whom we direct our acts of kindness reject our overtures, it is of no matter; we simply recognize such a moment as a further call to practice, a call to embody and extend loving-kindness to ourselves and to others (including the one who rebuffed our kindness), and thus to make our communities and our world more peaceful and just.

So, to practice in ways that honor the idea that "all life is interrelated," you might want to begin by asking yourself a few questions. In what areas of my life do I actively create community and in what areas do I reinforce a sense of separation and distance between others and me? When opportunities to connect deeply with or affirm others have arisen, did I embrace the opportunities or pass them up? Do I operate primarily from an "us" versus "them" framework, or even cast myself as a winner and others as losers? If so, have my personal "victories" actually made my life more peaceful, or have they bred distrust, resentment, and anger? ("In a battle," noted the Buddha, "the winners and the losers both lose.")[6]

From this line of inquiry, you can see where you have made interrelatedness the cornerstone of your thoughts, acts, and speech. Consequently, you can reinforce and ground yourself more deeply in your practice and thus remember more readily that whenever you "meet anyone," it is, as *A Course in Miracles* states, "a holy encounter."[7] You can also identify where you have made disconnection your truth. The point of this self-evaluation is not to judge yourself or to vilify every choice that you have made to separate from others. After all, when you carve out space from those who choose to be toxic, you honor and take great care of yourself. Instead, the point is to look at your intentions in order to see whether or not they are, in truth, simply a denial of our fundamental connection to each other, an embrace of "self" at the expense of "other." Ultimately, you must ask yourself: Are my intentions the stuff from which I can build a Beloved Community? Or am I just reinforcing ways of being that will inevitably reproduce a society marked by alienation and injustice?

The Whole Kingdom of Life

A self-examination such as this is, I believe, what King sought to inspire through his affirmation of interrelatedness, and thus he drove the issue home as often as he could. (Indeed, the statement "all life is interrelated" appears so frequently in King's speeches, essays, sermons, and books that it is safe to assume that it was a core tenet of his beliefs, including his belief in nonviolence.)[8]

Yet it is also clear that King sought to cast African Americans' nonviolent resistance as a selfless and heroic effort to reclaim from the violence of racism and segregation the truth that we are all connected to one another—to undo, in other words, the ways that racism and racist practices have estranged us all. As King saw it, this effort to reclaim our interrelatedness had the potential to heal the nation as a whole:

> The Negro in winning rights for himself produces substantial benefits for the nation. Just as a doctor will occasionally reopen a wound, because a dangerous infection hovers beneath the half-healed surface, the revolution for human rights is opening up unhealthy areas in American life and permitting a new and wholesome healing to take place. Eventually the civil-rights movement will have contributed infinitely more to the nation than the eradication of racial injustice. It will have enlarged the concept of brotherhood to a vision of total interrelatedness.[9]

Given the skepticism from the mainstream about movement tactics as well as outright opposition to rights for African Americans from whites vested in the racial order, King's effort to frame nonviolent resistance as a healing force that enlarges "the concept of brotherhood" and to explain interrelatedness on this basis is understandable. But his effort had this unintended consequence: it narrowed the broader meaning of his affirmation—a meaning that is critically important for us to take full-on as we traverse the path of nonviolence.

Let us look closely at King's statement that "all life is interrelated." Notice that it doesn't invite us to affirm merely our connection to one another as human beings. It invites us to do something that is much grander: to recognize that we are connected to *all* sentient beings, to Earth—to the whole of creation. "*All life* is interrelated" means precisely that, so in spite of King's own (understandably narrow) focus on *human* connection, he asks us also—intentionally or not—to touch Earth and to "kiss the sky," to see that we are caught up with them, with *all* of it, in "an inescapable network of mutuality." To paraphrase Howard Thurman, we belong "to life and the whole kingdom of life that includes all that lives and perhaps, also, all that has ever lived. In other words," we are "a part of a continuing, breathing, living existence."[10]

This much broader understanding of interrelatedness clearly requires that we *expand* the ethic of love—meaning, that we include within it other sentient beings and Earth or the natural environment. With "a boundless heart" we "should cherish all living beings," as the Buddha instructed in the *Metta Sutta*. We should radiate kindness everywhere and to all things, "upwards to the skies, and downwards to the depths; outwards and unbounded."[11]

Indeed, it would make little sense for us to practice nonviolence with one another and yet exclude from our practice all other forms of life and the planet that we inhabit. "Whatever affects one directly affects all indirectly" is no less true when applied to life writ large, as climate change and the crises it produces—and will continue to produce—make abundantly clear. It is incumbent upon us, therefore, to live our lives in ways that embody this idea, that project respect for the very ground that we and so many other beings traverse, and that honor each other's reliance on the sustenance that Earth provides. Doing so "will help us recognize," notes Thich Nhat Hanh, "the noblest nature in ourselves."[12]

We Have Loved Life

For African Americans, such a practice would actually be in keeping with the fact that we have always, as Alice Walker states, "loved life and loved the earth—though our relationship to the land and other sentient beings has certainly been transformed radically by our historic migrations from the South to Northern urban centers. For centuries, we forged deep connections with the natural environment that were sustaining and empowering for our communities. Through our farming, gardening, and healing practices, for instance, we developed an intimacy with Earth that allowed us to survive and thrive during difficult times. (As a case in point, black women who were slaves often "provided medical care on the plantation through their knowledge of wild remedies.")[13] Such intimacy in turn has enabled us to appreciate and understand Earth's resources and the power contained therein, and to use these for our benefit. It also enables us to understand that we need to replenish resources so that others might thrive. In addition, our intimacy with Earth makes us aware of our utter dependence on it for all things. This life-sustaining relationship to the land is one that many of us continue to nurture, including those of us who inhabit urban spaces.[14]

Earth has been and continues to be for African Americans a source of spiritual sustenance as well, a reminder to us that we are part of a grand creation extending through space and time.

Moreover, as we did in the past, we engage Earth as a partner in our spiritual practices (such as, for example, root-working and baptisms), and for many of us, Earth itself is a sacred, living being. With this awareness, we honor Earth accordingly, whether by the way we consciously walk on the planet or "notice" its beauty—as captured by Alice Walker through her character Shug in *The Color Purple:* "I think it pisses God off if you walk by the color purple in a field somewhere and don't notice it."[15] We also honor Earth as sacred by the way we resist—through political engagement—mindless acts that deplete, waste, and dirty Earth's resources; sicken and destroy entire species; and, of course, contaminate our own communities. "Environmental justice," wrote the organizers of the First National People of Color Environmental Leadership Summit, "affirms the sacredness of Mother Earth, ecological unity and the interdependence of all species, and the right to be free from ecological destruction."[16]

Finally, through our outdoor leisure activities (at the beaches, in city parks, on camping trips, during hikes, in our backyards), we renew and revitalize ourselves and therefore connect with our natural environment as a source of medicine for our health and mental well-being.

We also embraced our relationships with other sentient beings. Our early history in this country, in fact, is replete with folktales and fables—the Br'er Rabbit stories come to mind—which reveal just how much we saw ourselves "as part of a unified universe of all creatures." The stories reveal also that, as Mart A. Stewart observes, we "did not make a sharp distinction between humans and other creatures."[17] Instead, we related to them as family—indicated in the folktales by our characterization of animals (fox, bear, and rabbit, for example) as "Br'er," i.e., "brother." And in shaping our relationship with Earth, we obtained in the process knowledge about, as well as an intimacy with, other beings that have sustained us over time—whether in terms of physical survival, companionship, the pleasure in cocreating our habitats, or the simple joy of coexistence itself. This kind of intimacy has not been entirely lost as a result of migration and modernization.

So, it *is* true: We have loved life and loved the Earth, and loved them deeply— a legacy that many of us carry on in some measure in our day-to-day lives, and a legacy we actually share, in one way or another, with all of humanity. All of us have histories in which our forebears not only honored their intimate connections to the whole kingdom of life, but also understood and interpreted their existence through their relationships with Earth and its other inhabitants.

What's Love Got to Do with It?

It would be wonderful at this point to conclude that our relationship with Earth and other sentient beings has been and is all about love. Unfortunately, this is not the case. For many of us, nature is something to be tamed, mastered, and held at bay. Furthermore, being "out in nature"—in the forests, the deserts, the mountain ranges, for example—is an alien and threatening experience for some of us, one we'd rather leave to others and one that, in our view, is part of what defines the difference between "us" and "them." Although we have loved Earth and its myriad inhabitants, we have also treated them as other, and with all of the disregard (and, at times, violence) that that invites. Indeed, many subscribe to the particular view that animals are here only to serve us, and thus accord them treatment consistent with this belief. Climate change, global warming, species extinction: we have played some part in creating these catastrophes, even if we have done so from the margins of the economic and technological order. Of course, since what we say or do affects all life, then we have not escaped unscathed by the treatment that we have accorded Earth and its other beings.

Although there are myriad reasons why this is all true for so many of us, surely one of the most important is suggested by Alice Walker herself: African Americans' relationship to Earth and other sentient beings was and continues to be deeply scarred by our experiences within our nation's racial order, and most especially by the ways in which nature was (and continues to be) used to rationalize and facilitate racial subordination. Because these experiences might have affected our ability to affirm or even recognize our "total interrelatedness," we should take the time to reflect on them so that we might begin to transform these experiences for our benefit and the benefit of all life.

Consider, then, the following and ask yourself these questions: How might these experiences have shaped the ways that I engage nature (or don't)? Do they stand between me and the idea that all life is interrelated? How have the choices I made as a result of knowing about these experiences affected Earth and other beings?

- The definition of African Americans within our founding Constitution as three-fifths human
- The historical construction of African Americans as beasts and as primitives, in order to justify slavery, Jim Crow, and, arguably, mass incarceration
- The brutal use of African American children, women, and men to extract Earth's resources and abundance (agricultural slave labor, sharecropping) for the benefit of white landowners and communities
- The exclusion, throughout most of American history, of African Americans from land and resource ownership (the broken promise of forty acres and a mule, for example)
- The use of nature—trees, forests, rivers, lakes, other sentient beings—to carry out acts of racist violence (such as lynching)
- The demarcation of land as "colored" and "white" in order to reinforce white supremacy over space, natural resources, and even other living beings
- The often violent exclusion of African Americans, again throughout most of American history, from natural environments preserved and set aside for public leisure
- The vast migration of African Americans from the South to the concrete spaces of Northern

> urban centers, driven in great measure by the violence of the Jim Crow system and the peonage that was sharecropping

Through your examination of this list, you might find that some of these experiences resonate in terms of your relationship to, and engagement with, both the natural environment and other beings. They are wounds, in other words, that mark your experiences in the natural world and that have created for you a sense of disconnection from so much that lies within "the whole kingdom of life."

When I was a child, my family made frequent excursions from Buffalo, New York, to a small steel town in Pennsylvania, where my grandparents lived. I loved those road trips because we had to wind our way through the beautiful Allegheny Mountains. On those long drives I'd try my best to stay awake so that I might get the chance to spot a deer or some other wild creature standing among the pines. I'd fantasize about the day I would be free to live on my own, in the woods, conversing with animals who would visit me frequently at my log cabin. Never did it occur to me that I would feel unsafe or be vulnerable to violence.

That changed as I got older. Though the fantasy of a Thoreau-like existence is one that I have never abandoned, it has nevertheless been tempered by my having heard, over and over, my parents' warning—often when I mentioned plans to venture out beyond city limits—that I needed to be careful because "there are crazy people out there" (I understood that by "crazy people" they meant white people, and primarily men); by stories that I heard and/or read that retold acts of racist violence that African Americans frequently experienced in the woods and other landscapes; by my own rare encounters with other African Americans in the wilds; and by the surprised and sometimes unwelcoming looks on the faces of whites whom I've encountered on hiking trails, by secluded lakes, and at camping sites.

I go to the woods, nevertheless, because I love them, because this creation never ceases to amaze me. But at times, I do so with history as my companion. Sometimes, it affects whether I go off-trail, or how deeply; sometimes it eggs me on, reminding me just how familiar my ancestors were with such spaces, and how much they "loved Earth."

Then there are those times when I won't venture at all; times when either someone is in fact "out there" armed with weapons and rage, or history, to paraphrase William Wordsworth, is "too much" with me, such that there is "little" that I "see in Nature that is ours."[18] (How much of this disconnect, I wonder, has to do with my having to traverse, more often than not, segregated spaces in order to enter "protected" wooded areas?)

The African American "relationship to the woods, and most other natural lands," write Cassandra Y. Johnson and Josh McDaniel, "emerged from a context of exploitation that presently informs the African American relationship to wildlands."[19] *My* relationship to the wildlands certainly bears witness to this fact, and maybe you have a story that bears witness as well—like the one told, for instance, by a nineteen-year-old who was interviewed for research on African Americans' use of national parks. She doesn't visit such places, she confessed, because her "granddaddy" told her that "the K.K.K. hangs out up in the mountains."[20]

How many of us have grown up on such stories and have consequently foregone an opportunity to hang out "up in the mountains" or in other natural spaces? And what have we lost—what have we *missed*—as a result? Indeed, what have Earth and other beings lost or missed as a result of our absence?

Just as the African American relationship to woods and other lands emerged from a context of exploitation, so also did our relationship to animals. "New World slavery," observes Melissa Harris-Perry,

> did not consider enslaved Africans to be conquered persons, but to be chattel, beast[s] of burden, fully subhuman and therefore not requiring the basic rights of humans. By defining slaves as animals and then abusing them horribly the American slave system degraded both black people and animals. By equating black people to animals it both asserted the superiority of humans to animals, arrayed some humans (black people) as closer to animals and therefore less human, and implied that all subjugated persons and all animals could be used and abused at the will of those who were more powerful. The effects were pernicious for both black people and for animals.[21]

None of this ended with slavery, as Harris-Perry explains further, and African Americans continue to be equated with animals in the public sphere—particularly in discourse on crime—as well as subjected to racial subordination. Moreover, our society is one in which animal abuse and oppression have been normalized.

Yet we have been and are complicit in the ill treatment of animals. Whereas most of us are passive participants in this treatment (through, for example, our consumption choices—food, beauty products, medicines), some of us are active participants, and at times in ways that are extreme and brutal (dog fighting, for example). Our complicity signifies a disconnection that not only denies the interrelatedness of all life; it also, ironically, rationalizes our own abuse and oppression. For as Harris-Perry observes, "when the abuse and oppression of an entire group of people is justified as acceptable because they are defined as animals, then it stands to reason the society is suggesting that abuse and oppression are acceptable ways to treat animals." Again, since all life is interrelated, the harm that we visit upon animals—whether or not it proceeds from the context of exploitation—is inevitably harm that we visit upon ourselves.

Clearly, our connection to "all life" is just as much in need of healing and of reclamation as is our connection to other human beings. It is not enough, therefore, to mend only the relationship that we have with one another. Our relationship to the planet and the rest of its inhabitants requires medicine as well—medicine that we must be willing to administer if we are to embody and demonstrate fully that *all* life is interrelated.

A New and Wholesome Healing

A great way for us to begin to reclaim our interrelatedness is by first recognizing this truth: that wherever we go, there Earth is. It is an obvious fact, but one that perhaps many of us need to see with new eyes since most of us live in urban spaces, some of which are "greened," some of which are block after block of cement broken up by the occasional tree or patch of grass (if we're lucky). In such environments, it is easy to forget and, consequently, to be alienated from the fact that there is soil and teeming life beneath our feet.

But why start here? For this simple reason: If we never get out to the woods or go to a beach or camp in a national park (as Oprah did in 2010 for the first time in her life when she camped in Yosemite)[22] or visit a desert when its flowers are in full bloom—if we never venture beyond a ten-block radius—we can still move and breathe with the awareness that we are situated on Earth and are thus *completely* connected to and in touch with the sacred. This awareness must necessarily shift how we engage with our planet and see our surroundings, as well as how we see ourselves, for by consciously and reverently touching the earth, we remind ourselves that we belong *to* Earth and thus belong *everywhere*, as do all other beings we encounter—human or otherwise. (The notion that we belong everywhere, of course, is a truth that African Americans have needed to reclaim for quite some time, especially since it is one that segregation—both de jure *and* de facto—has denied and continues to deny.) Since "whatever affects one directly affects all indirectly," we end up extending to Earth and its inhabitants the benefits of our shift in perspective. We exchange, in other words, a sense of the sacred with everyone and everything around us because we see clearly that we absolutely belong to one another.

When I walk the city streets, I try to remember to slow my pace and practice what in Buddhism is referred to as "walking meditation." For every step that I take, I focus my attention on the feel of my foot touching concrete (which I imagine to be an entry point, not a barrier, to the soil beneath); the movement of my body through space; and the rhythm of my breath. With each step, I repeat to myself, "touching the earth, the earth touches me,"[23] and I do this until I am no longer someone caught up in the hustle and bustle of city life, lost to random thoughts about work or what I'm going to cook for dinner, and disconnected from both the life around me and the ground beneath my feet. Slowing down, I become present and fully aware of the planet itself, aware of it as that to which we are all connected—including the pigeon that I might have, just moments ago and with great disdain, shooed out of my way.

My sense of place expands, in other words, as does my sense of connection. Suddenly, I am able to notice and enjoy a neighbor's garden, discern the love and care with which he tended the earth. Because I no longer take up space with stress and worry, no one has to scurry out of my path in order to avoid the possibility of a collision. I fill space instead with lightness and joy. Such is the gift of reconnecting—even through concrete—with Earth itself. The "future of all life, including our own," writes Thich Nhat Hanh, "depends on our mindful steps."[24]

The other part of the gift is this: I can still make this

connection even as I continue to negotiate the hazards and dangers of walking city streets. Street harassment does not go away simply because I have decided to touch the earth. I still have to watch out for drivers for whom traffic rules are mere suggestions. Because I hear gunshots on a regular basis in my neighborhood, I still have to keep my eyes and ears wide open. The police, at any moment, could swarm in from all directions, weapons drawn, making it unsafe for many of us to be outdoors at all.

In a sense, nothing changes.

On the other hand, *everything* changes. *I* shift—in mind, body, and spirit—because part of the power in connecting to Earth in such spaces and under such circumstances is that it is both an affirmation, in spite of it all, of one's belongingness to creation writ large and a refusal to be or see oneself as trapped in one's small world—or in anyone else's small world, for that matter. It is a refusal to see myself and others only in terms of the narrow and too-often dangerous confines of the street, the block, or the neighborhood. I trust that such a shift on my part changes, even if only in some small way, everything and everyone around me. At the very least, I am able to walk with some measure of joy even when everything (and, at times, someone) suggests that I should do otherwise.

If this practice is too challenging, then as you walk you can instead simply notice every tree, bush, and flower that you pass. Notice even the grass and weeds pushing through the cracks of the sidewalk. Take a moment and look up at the sky from time to time, and let the spaciousness of it remind you that Earth is your home.

We can also reclaim our interrelatedness by celebrating the ways that the natural environment and other beings gave comfort to and sustained the lives of our ancestors. The Ku Klux Klan might very well have hung out in the mountains—and maybe they still do—but so, also, did our great-great-grandmothers. While there, they hunted, fished, found spiritual renewal, and, at times, liberated themselves. It was through the Appalachian and Allegheny Mountains, after all, that many of them walked to gain their freedom.

It is a mistake for us to forget these stories, for to do so is to banish from our awareness not only the complexity of our ancestors' relationship with the land and other life forms, but also the power that they did exercise—through their engagement in and with the natural world—under truly extraordinary circumstances. Armed with only part of the story, we run the risk of prescribing for ourselves a narrow vision of our place on the planet, thereby surrendering our own power as well as our birthright, which is our belongingness to all life.

If you think about it, you will see that the stories themselves are actually great medicine. They let us know how deeply connected we always have been and are to the natural order. They thus reveal the essence of who we are—an essence that can never be distorted by structures of subordination or even our own limited and diminished perception of ourselves and others. The stories tell us as well that Earth and its other inhabitants have always been and are witnesses to our grander existence, as we have been witnesses for them. So it is important that we remember our ancestors' *whole* relationship to all life. By so doing, we engage in a practice that helps us to heal whatever ways we are alienated from the natural world and, consequently, from ourselves.

Reconcile "with the past," therefore, "and then move forward to reclaim and reacquaint" yourself with the "forests and woodlands" in which your "forebears both learned and survived," as Cassandra Y. Johnson and Josh McDaniel encourage us all to do.[25] If you are able, go on a walk or a hike, camp out, fish, or just sit still and enjoy the quiet. Notice the movement and sounds of the woodlands' residents. Let them reveal to you their secrets. Then go and do the same in the deserts, on mountain ranges, at the banks of our rivers. Or even in your neighborhood park.

Allow yourself to be at home.

We can reclaim our connection, too, by celebrating our own culturally unique relationships with the natural world. From within the "context of exploitation," as Colin Fisher observes, we have managed to carve out space in which to interact with nature and other beings on our own terms. In other words, we have always "sought nature," though we "frequently had to overcome racism, de facto segregation, and sometimes violence" in order to enjoy it.[26] Understanding this, we can strengthen our relationships, and can do so by intentionally redefining them—through our thoughts, words, and deeds—as the stuff upon which a nonviolent and just society depends. In this way, we make the act of cherishing "all living beings" as well as Earth the very meaning and measure of justice.

Thus, take a look at the ways that you have sought nature.

Do they reflect your family's and your community's practices, and if so, how far back can you trace them? Have the spaces that you use and enjoy always been available to African Americans? If not, what did your family and the members of your community do to make these spaces accessible for all? How would your answers change your perspective and your behavior?

By thinking these issues through, you ground yourself and your engagement with nature in a broader history of resistance and affirmation. You can then begin to align your intention to seek out and be in nature with your vision of a just society.

Finally, in order to heal our relationship with animals and other beings, we need to consider that maybe we have got it all wrong, that maybe "the animals of the world" actually exist not for us but "for their own reasons," as Alice Walker has stated. They were not, in other words, "made for humans any more than black people were made for white people, or women created for men."[27] We should ponder why we have considered "life as it appears" in other beings "so different from life as it appears in a human," and face the costs to us and to all life of embracing this belief. Has "our feeling of separateness from other life forms," as Sharon Salzberg has asked, actually brought us "joy and a sense of wholeness?"[28] From such reflections, we may be moved to reconsider how we eat, what we wear, how we treat the animals that we live with or the ones whom we encounter daily, how we invest, where we spend our money, and even whom we support for political office.

Because practices like these transform the self/other

division engendered by the "context of exploitation," they ultimately put us in nonviolent relationship with other sentient beings and the natural environment. Just as significantly, they also transform the self/other division that has manifested from our own willing participation in the production of a culture that has privileged consumerism and resource depletion at great cost to Earth, to other species, and to ourselves. Consequently, we are compelled to engage in acts of noncooperation with such violence, whether in terms of our everyday choices around food, travel, and livelihood, or in terms of our broader political and economic activity. In any case, we project the ethic of love to the center of our lives and thus make nonviolence, through the ways that we engage with the natural world, our everyday lived experience. And by leaving nothing out of our affirmation that all life is interrelated, we manifest a broader ecology of justice.

A Dream

To some degree, we can think of the civil rights movement itself and our triumph over de jure racial segregation as a beginning of sorts in our efforts to reclaim our connection with all life. For through our activism and resistance, we gained access to parks, beaches, and other recreation areas from which we were excluded. Moreover, we consciously included such natural spaces within our vision of a just society as well as expressed our intention to reclaim them from the racial order. Though not articulated specifically in the original commitment card, this intention was nevertheless a driving force behind the Birmingham Campaign, as King suggested through his discussion of that action as an outgrowth of African American life in Bull Connor's Birmingham:

> If your powers of imagination were great enough to enable you to place yourself in the position of a Negro . . . born and brought up . . . in Birmingham, you would have pictured your life in the following manner: [. . .] You would spend your childhood playing mainly in the streets because the "colored" parks were abysmally inadequate. When a federal court order banned park segregation, you would find that Birmingham closed down its parks and gave up its baseball team rather than integrate them.[29]

In even broader strokes, King gave voice in his "I Have a Dream" speech—delivered just months after the Birmingham Campaign—to our intention to reclaim natural spaces. Specifically, he reimagined the nation's landscape—"the prodigious hilltops of New Hampshire," "the mighty mountains of New York," "the heightening Alleghenies of Pennsylvania," "the snowcapped Rockies of Colorado," "the curvaceous slopes of California," "Stone Mountain of Georgia," "Lookout Mountain of Tennessee," and "every hill and molehill of Mississippi"—as a landscape expressive *not* of racial subordination, but instead of "total interrelatedness." All of "God's children," King proclaimed, would someday "be able to join hands" everywhere and across the land.

Given statements such as these, I am willing to believe that even though King spoke of total interrelatedness solely in human terms, he understood it to be something much more, something that absolutely expands not only our concept of justice, but also what it means to live a life of nonviolence.

What it means is this: For our brief time on this wonderful planet, we must bow deeply to one another, to Earth, and to all other sentient beings, and resist with the power of love anything that creates or stands as a barrier between ourselves and the whole kingdom of life.

5 Strive to Be in Good Bodily Health

I have experienced personally over the past few years how a purity of diet and thought are interrelated. And when Americans become truly concerned with the purity of the food that enters their own personal systems, when they learn to eat properly, we can expect to see profound changes effected in the social and political system of this nation. The two systems are inseparable.

—Dick Gregory[1]

The Black Body

By far the most intriguing commitment of the Birmingham Campaign's pledge card is the ninth: "Strive to be in good spiritual and bodily health." At first blush, it appears to have been something of an afterthought—a commitment that organizers added when they realized that they forgot to include the body as part of volunteers' nonviolent practice. Admittedly, the card's preamble is one through which volunteers affirmed they would commit their persons and their bodies to the campaign. It is likely, however, that that affirmation had more to do with volunteers promising that they would face violence without retaliation than it had to do with securing their vow to adopt a healthful diet and lifestyle.

Buttressing the sense that the ninth commitment was an afterthought is the fact that it is the last explicitly *aspirational* pledge (the tenth simply charged volunteers to follow campaign organizers' directions)—and somewhat redundant. After all, the eight prior commitments are, for all intents and purposes, practices that were offered to help volunteers achieve "good . . . spiritual health."

However, the ninth commitment's focus on good *bodily* health makes it not simply the most intriguing of the commitments, but also one of the most far-reaching, and thus one that organizers clearly included with great purpose. Consider this: By implying that good bodily health would be both an expression of volunteers' vow of nonviolence and a means by which they would topple the system of segregation, the ninth commitment provided a framework through which volunteers could think more broadly *and radically* about the care that they accorded their bodies. It was a framework, in fact, that subtly presented to volunteers the challenge of examining how their day-to-day self-care related to their embrace of nonviolence as a strategy and way of life, and to their pursuit of justice.

Now, whether or not organizers consciously intended the ninth commitment to offer this challenge, I cannot say. More likely than not, organizers specifically hoped to convey to volunteers that since they were going to engage in activities that would make them targets of physical violence and deprivation, it was crucial for them to take great care of their bodies: i.e., to counter with self-love (eating healthful foods, exercising, finding ways to minimize stress, for example) the violence that they would face throughout the campaign.

Furthermore, organizers may have intended to teach the invaluable lesson that although nonviolence is a practice that compels one to confront power and to face the violent consequences of so doing, it is nevertheless a practice and a way of life expressive of one's profound love and respect for the body. Nonviolence simply asks us to refuse to make the *fear* of bodily harm and even death an obstacle to our pursuit of justice, a fear upon which the purveyors of violence and injustice depend. As Howard Thurman framed it, it is "important in the etiquette of violence that the fear [of violence] be centered around one's physical life and well-being or that of one's loved ones. By every cunning contrivance and subtlety, emphasis must be placed upon *physical* existence as the supreme good. . . . Once this is established, the only thing remaining for violence is to threaten to kill. If the highest premium is placed upon life, the fear of its loss or injury enables violence to maintain itself in active control over the lives of others. If there is no fear of this point, then the power of violence is critically undermined."[2]

Even if I cannot be entirely certain about the Birmingham Campaign organizers' purpose for including bodily health as part of volunteers' commitment to the campaign, what I *can* say is that the ninth commitment's challenge is one African Americans—indeed, all people of conscience—must take on as their own. In fact, when we consider the myriad health issues that many families and communities face (heart disease, cancer, diabetes, and homicide, just to give a few examples), the disparities in health outcomes for African Americans, as well as the conditions that produce many of these health issues, it is clearly incumbent upon us to love our bodies unconditionally both as an end in itself *and* as our intentional commitment to, and day-to-day practice of, nonviolence. In the process, we will come to understand self-care and thus self-love not only as resistance to injustice, but also as a powerful means to create a more just society.

How to begin? We can take stock of our health and health practices by examining them through the lens of nonviolence: i.e., through our dedication to do no harm to others or to ourselves. This will allow us to situate our practices within a larger context, to see that how we care for ourselves (the everyday choices that we make regarding health, diets, physical fitness) has political, economic, social, and spiritual consequences that touch more lives than our own.

Consider, for example, the choice that many of us make to drink coffee as part of our daily diet. To fuel our habit (it is one that I indulge regularly), many poor countries have dedicated more of their arable land to coffee production and less to crops that can feed their own people. Coffee production itself contributes to the degradation of these countries' natural environments, whether by way of producers' destruction of forests to increase coffee yields, contamination of waterways by coffee-processing plants, or the generation of waste that damages soil. Moreover, many of those who labor to give us the coffee that we enjoy do not do so freely; indeed, our morning cup might well have been made possible by slave and child labor.[3]

Truths such as these make clear that we are called upon to make choices about our health that are simultaneously and fundamentally expressions of care for others and for the planet. Such facts also challenge us to free ourselves from the narrow, individual-oriented framework by which we have been encouraged to think about our health—a framework that ultimately does not serve us or the rest of the world.

Practice: The Fifth Mindfulness Training

Aware of the suffering caused by unmindful consumption, I am committed to cultivating good health, both physical and mental, for myself, my family, and my society by practicing mindful eating, drinking, and consuming. I will ingest only items that preserve peace, well-being, and joy in my body, in my consciousness, and in the collective body and consciousness of my family and society. I am determined not to use alcohol or any other intoxicant or to ingest foods or other products that contain toxins, such as certain TV programs, magazines, books, films, and conversations. I am aware that to damage my body or my consciousness with these poisons is to betray my ancestors, my parents, my society, and future generations. I will work to transform violence, fear, anger, and confusion in myself and in society by practicing a diet for myself and for society. I understand that a proper diet is crucial for self-transformation and for the transformation of society.[4]

This last of the five Mindfulness Trainings developed by Buddhist monk Thich Nhat Hanh in order to help laypeople traverse "the path of right understanding and true love, leading to healing, transformation, and happiness for ourselves and for the world" is, I think, a wonderful guide for our self-examination.[5] Not only does it prod us gently to examine the "suffering caused by unmindful consumption"; it also, at the same time, directs us to adopt an ethic of self-care and, more broadly, an ethic of consumption that brings peace to our bodies and minds as well as to "the collective body and consciousness" of our families and society. This is work that we want to do, whether or not we are Buddhist, because it grounds us in a concern for, and in a deep commitment to, the well-being of all sentient beings and thus to peace itself. Moreover, such work captures beautifully what a nonviolent approach to and viewpoint on our health practices might actually look like.

Thus, let us track carefully this Fifth Mindfulness Training so that we can begin to radicalize our health practices, to remake them into instruments by which we realize nonviolence as a way of life as well as to restructure our society into one more in line with our ethic of love.

Aware of the suffering caused by unmindful consumption, I am committed to cultivating good health, both physical and mental, for myself, my family, and my society by practicing mindful eating, drinking, and consuming.

"Unmindful consumption"—eating and drinking, as well as consuming nonfood products without regard to their ill-effects on us, on other sentient beings, on Earth—is so normalized and encouraged in our society that we might at first find it difficult to bring to mind specific examples of unmindful consumption, let alone the suffering that it can create.

We are, for instance, bombarded by commercials and ads that feature beautiful, healthy, and happy people who are apparently beautiful, healthy, and happy because they eat food that is processed, fattening, permeated by hormones and, more likely than not, genetically modified. In reality, millions of people suffer the terrible costs of eating such food—hypertension, obesity, cancer, early puberty, diabetes. Our food is packaged in ways that suggest that it is produced in idyllic circumstances instead of under frightening and oppressive conditions. Though the chickens we eat, for instance, may have never walked more than two feet in their entire lives or enjoyed the open air because they're warehoused by the thousands in cramped, filthy conditions, they are nevertheless presented to us in wrapping that depicts a spacious country farm, a place where the chickens (we are led to believe) roamed free under clear blue skies. Or how about this? The stylish clothes that we are encouraged to buy and that are presented to us by thin, beautiful fashion models are by and large produced by poor women of color, often under brutal sweatshop conditions. We are fed a steady diet of commercials that encourage us to eat meat regularly—with every meal, if we can—yet meat consumption contributes to the creation of greenhouse gases that are heating our atmosphere, transforming our climate, and threatening life on Earth.[6]

These are, tragically, just a few examples of how we are encouraged from various quarters to consume without thought, worry, or critical analysis, and to eat, drink, and "ingest" nonfood items without troubling ourselves about the harmful consequences of our consumption on our bodies, on the bodies of other sentient beings, or to Earth itself. Our challenge, therefore, is not simply to cultivate good health, but to do so by becoming aware of unmindful consumption in our personal lives and in society at large, so that we might purposively confront it with the intention to make mindful consumption the norm and transform through nonviolent resistance practices that have caused so much suffering.

What, then, is the quality of the consciousness that you bring to your consumption choices? Do you know, for example, what is in the food you eat? Have you ever investigated the ingredients with which you are unfamiliar? Do you know what food is good for you, and why?

Cultivating good health, especially in these days of additives, the injection of hormones into livestock, and the genetic modification of plant-based foods, necessarily means that we have to become vigilant about the food we eat so that we don't find ourselves consuming items that actually harm. When we consume unmindfully, we surrender to others responsibility for *our* health. This is a tricky business, for, as Adama Maweja notes, "the business interests" of food and beverage industries "have, at their heart, the idea of profit instead of genuine concern for the well-being and health of people, children, and the sustainability of the earth."[7] Given this, do we really want to leave our health in their hands? Do we really want to surrender our power?

As you conduct your self-assessment, you should also take

time to reflect on how your consumption affects the planet as well as other sentient beings. Do you ever think about how your food is produced? How the animals that you eat are treated, or whether it makes sense—physically, ethically—to eat animals at all? Have you ever considered the lives of the people who harvested your food or the political interests served by the food made available to you?

Awareness of these kinds of connections is, as Martin Luther King Jr. argues, crucial to our ability to create a peaceful world. "Did you ever stop to think that you can't leave for your job in the morning without being dependent on most of the world?" King wrote. "You get up in the morning and go to the bathroom and reach over for the sponge, and that's handed to you by a Pacific islander. You reach for a bar of soap, and that's given to you at the hands of a Frenchman. And then you go into the kitchen to drink your coffee for the morning, and that's poured into your cup by a South American. . . . And before you finish eating breakfast in the morning, you've depended on more than half of the world. . . . We aren't going to have peace on earth until we recognize this basic fact of the interrelated structure of all reality."[8]

But it is not simply our failure to recognize our dependence "on half the world" for our breakfast that undermines peace. It is our failure to recognize that, as a consequence of our unmindfulness or lack of awareness, we end up tacitly supporting the exploitation and violence that are often put to service in order to make our breakfast possible. Consuming unmindfully, in other words, constitutes a failure to look deeply into everything that has gone into making possible the food on our plates or the clothes on our backs or the petroleum in our cars. Blissfully unaware, we sustain and nurture injustice abroad. Blissfully unaware, then, we sow the seeds of distrust, resentment, and rage.

For this part of the training, then, we make a commitment to wake up, to become aware, and then to act from our awareness. This means that we not only "practice mindful eating, drinking, and consuming," but also that we embrace the responsibility to create, through purposeful, nonviolent action, the conditions in which real peace can flourish.

I will ingest only items that preserve peace, well-being, and joy in my body, in my consciousness, and in the collective body and consciousness of my family and society.

When you vow to ingest items that "preserve peace," you make a commitment to notice how the things that you consume affect your body and consciousness. That is, you notice not only the items that make you feel at ease, but you pay attention to those that make you suffer and especially make you feel anything but peaceful.

Take a look at what happens after you have consumed your favorite foods and drinks. Do you feel lethargic, uncomfortable, depressed, irritable, restless, aggressive, or angry? If so, what do you do with that energy? Are your interactions with family members, friends, or the people in your community affected as a result? Just as importantly, how do you treat *yourself* after you have consumed such items?

On occasion, I will eat foods loaded with spices, knowing full well that I will pay later on with heartburn and indigestion. Invariably, I'll become irritated, grumpy, and edgy as a result. Now, my choice to eat spicy food would be all well and good if I lived by myself on an island. I could suffer alone, as it were. But such is not the case. Consequently, everyone around me pays the cost for the choice that I made. I'll get angry over small things, touchy, and generally impossible to live with. And all of this usually happens without my realizing that there is any connection between what I ate and my behavior.

This is hardly surprising. Scientific research demonstrates a connection between diet and emotions. Scientists believe, for example, a correlation may exist between deficiencies in omega-3 fatty acids, commonly found in flax seeds, and aggression and hostility.[9] Thus, we would do well to pay attention to the ways our foods affect us both physically and emotionally.

Whereas this part of the training most certainly draws your attention to how your body and mind react to, or are affected by, what you ingest, it also nudges you to ask: If by my consumption choices I am not preserving peace but instead cultivating dis-ease or harm, then am I not simply participating in and colluding with those who, for profit, disregard the health and well-being of all of us? Have I not adopted an ethic of violence toward my body and, by extension, toward my family members as well as people in my community?

Through such inquiries, we see that what we ingest has consequences beyond the effects on our own health. Indeed, they ripple outward, so that we end up not only poisoning ourselves but our relations and interactions with others, even if only briefly. How much strife in our homes and communities, we should wonder, can be traced to what we ingest and to our overall health practices?

We should also consider the possibility that our food choices may reflect our lack of self-love and regard for our own bodies, a lack that for African Americans in particular is part and parcel of the disregard we face on a daily basis. Or to put it more bluntly, through our questions we might find just how much we have become—or how much we have willingly made ourselves—instruments of those who profit from and thus reinforce our poor health practices.

To the extent that this is our truth, we need to come to a place where we can say, as Fannie Lou Hamer did years ago, that we are "sick and tired of being sick and tired." Though Hamer was speaking to just how fed up African Americans were with the system of segregation and racism as a whole, her statement nevertheless is one that we might need to claim as a means to focus our attention on the possibility that what we consume and the ways that we care for our bodies are haunted by (and collude with) the legacies of slavery and segregation, as they are also marked by our experiences of present-day racism and racist practices. (The Nation of Islam's longstanding claim that soul food is "slave food" was motivated in part by its recognition of the connections between our diets and racial subordination.)

"We must come to terms with the fact that the foods we've grown accustomed to—that have even helped to create the concept of our ethnic identity—may actually be feeding the machine of neocolonialism," writes A. Breeze Harper, and "that we remain enslaved to a system that thrives on our addictions and mental, physical, and emotional illnesses."[10] Thinking of our consumption in this way, we see that we must both liberate our bodies from diets that make us sick and tired, steeped as they are in a politics of oppression and violence, and refuse to be collaborators in our own suffering.

Finally, this part of the training encourages all of us to consider more broadly whether the nonfood items that we enjoy—movies, Internet sites, television shows, and so on—constitute consumption that is also grounded in an ethic of violence. It suggests that what we eat, what we read, and what we watch—all of it—can cultivate and reinforce either violence or peace. Thus, we should look closely at whether or not our consumption of nonfood items brings us any peace of mind or, for that matter, peace of body. If you find that certain things that you enjoy make you agitated, edgy, angry, or affect you in other disturbing ways, then you might want to rethink your consumption of them.

"There are far reaching consequences to changing our lifestyle, diet, and habits," writes Maweja. When we realize that these include "better health; more clarity, potency, power, and peace; and greater ethical and moral consistency, as well as the redistribution of the wealth that we make and receive," then the choice of whether or not to "ingest only items that preserve peace, well-being, and joy" becomes a much easier choice for us to make.[11]

I am determined not to use alcohol or any other intoxicant, or to ingest foods or other items that contain toxins, such as certain TV programs, magazines, books, films, and conversations. I am aware that to damage my body or my consciousness with these poisons is to betray my ancestors, my parents, my society, and future generations.

It is certainly true that many kinds of "foods or other items" cloud our minds and poison our bodies, and in so doing affect our ability to think and to act from a place of reflection, clarity, and discernment. Yet, it is also clear that *we ourselves* can be toxic. We can poison our families and communities with the kinds of conversations that we engage in, or by how we act as well as treat others. We can also be poisoned by supporting someone else's toxicity, like egging on another's propensity to gossip or to complain. Consequently, whereas we might very well choose to embrace a healthful diet and refrain from using alcohol or other intoxicants, these are of no matter if we engage regularly in conversations that harm instead of heal, or if we adopt a steady diet of, for example, Internet sites that appeal to our lesser selves. Ultimately, we are simply putting a healthy veneer—like the pretty packaging by which many corporations wrap their unhealthful products—over our toxicity.

Through this part of the training, then, we state our intention not only to refrain from ingesting toxins, but also to commit to being a source of health and healing in our homes and in our communities. We ask ourselves such questions as: To what extent do I offer to others healing and help? How often do I choose instead to contribute to conflict and stress in my family, in my work environment, or in my community? What am I ingesting on a regular basis that feeds my propensity to act in toxic ways?

From these questions, we allow ourselves to wonder, as Charles Johnson does, just "what it would be like to live in a society where, instead of men and women insulting and tearing each other down, people in their social relations, and even in the smallest ways, held the highest intellectual, moral, creative, and spiritual expectations for one another."[12] We imagine ourselves in such a society—indeed, as one of its cocreators—so that we might practice in the present moment the kind of citizenship that such a society requires and, as a consequence, honor our ancestors, parents, society, and future generations. By choosing to refrain from ingesting toxins and being toxic, we can act with the kind of clarity and discernment that will enable us to heal the harms that our poisons have caused for ourselves and for others, and put an end to whatever practices we have in place—whether in our homes or in some corporate boardroom—that will surely visit great harm and suffering on future generations.

I will work to transform violence, fear, anger, and confusion in myself and in society by practicing a diet for myself and for society. I understand that a proper diet is crucial for self-transformation and for the transformation of society.

The work of the Fifth Training really asks us to come to terms with how we have, through our diets, cultivated within ourselves "violence, fear, anger, and confusion." That is, we face squarely the connections between consumption and violence, in both our personal lives and in society as a whole, so we might purposively make nonviolence and peace the basis for how we eat as well as consume nonfood items. Therefore, in sealing our self-assessment, we ask ourselves whether or not what we eat serves peace, whether or not what we read cultivates nonviolence, and whether or not what we wear contributes to the well-being of others and of the planet.

To those areas of our self-care that proceed from an ethic of violence, we lovingly turn and meet with acts of noncooperation. We make ourselves, in other words, objects to which we apply nonviolent resistance.

At first blush, this might seem counterintuitive, given that nonviolent action has customarily focused on systems and institutional agents. But the truth is that nonviolence requires us to confront violence wherever it expresses itself, and that must necessarily include the violence within—whether that be the violence of our society (which we have, to borrow Allen Aubrey Boesak's phrasing, turned "onto ourselves") or the violence that we have turned "*into* ourselves, allowing its pernicious presence to inhabit our minds and, unavoidably, our souls."[13] To challenge warmongering and yet to leave undisturbed our own violence is an unsustainable contradiction, one that ultimately compromises, if not undercuts entirely, our ability to put an end to war. To be at peace, we must put everything on the table.

Turning inward, then, you might exercise "love in action" by, for example, adopting a healthful diet, exercising, becoming a vegetarian, meditating daily, turning off the television, or undertaking other actions that express your resolve to transform your ethic of violence into an ethic of love. It's important not to make these changes from a place of shame or blame, from a belief that something is wrong with you or that you have to conform to some unattainable idea of health and beauty that has caused so many people to suffer. You cannot turn yourself into "the enemy," in other words, for to do so is to collude with violence and to make it your own. Instead, you make changes from both your commitment to all sentient beings and your desire to be a source of healing and peace. Noncooperation, after all, is nothing less than an expression of love and care, both for others *and* for you.

Radical Reconstruction

Integral to our self-directed practice of noncooperation is our willingness to meet with resistance the purveyors of harmful health and consumption, as well as the political institutions that support them. It is not enough simply to change our own personal health practices, for we are, in truth, called upon to root out and provide alternatives to a culture of consumption in which our health and the health of all sentient beings are given short shrift. Our self-directed noncooperation, then, is only a first step, one that provides us with the conviction necessary to meet this larger challenge.

Therefore, we should tune in to and participate in the conversations, critiques, and political actions targeting (both locally and globally) what are, in essence, assaults upon our health. Whether we confront the proliferation of food deserts and fast-food chains in poor communities; the exploitation of farmworkers; neoliberal policies that foster inequality and thus hunger throughout the world; the power of agribusiness to determine the kinds of foods made available to us; or the marketing of fattening, unhealthy foods to African American communities, we need to speak up and put our bodies on the line, and with the consciousness that a "radical reconstruction of society" (to use Martin Luther King Jr.'s words) into one premised on and invested in the health and well-being of all of Earth's inhabitants, is precisely what this moment calls for.

But how can we effectively move forward on this if we are, by and large, sick and tired? Clearly, the high incidents of diabetes, cancer, obesity, heart disease, high blood pressure, and other debilitating health issues within our communities necessarily have *huge* repercussions on our ability to be actively involved citizens who are fully engaged in speaking truth to power as well as in transforming the violence in our families, communities, and society at large. Dietary habits, for example, might be forcing some of us to spend an inordinate amount of time, energy, and material resources on managing chronic illness and pain—resources that could have been devoted to getting involved in, say, a neighborhood-organizing effort to address police misconduct. If this is the case, then such dietary habits stand in the way of our effectuating the radical reconstruction of society that King envisioned and that remains a necessary pursuit, as these chronic health issues make abundantly clear.

So ask yourself this: Have health issues kept me from being

actively involved in my community or engaged in addressing critical political issues? Would I be involved in the concerns of my community if I were healthier?

A Healthy Beloved Community

The Birmingham Campaign commitment card's directive to strive for good bodily health contains not only a challenge to think more radically about the relationship between self-care and justice; it also contains the challenge to imagine Beloved Community through the prism of health. In particular, the ninth commitment invites us to see Beloved Community as a group of citizens who embody both spiritual and physical wellness.

But let's go a step further. The commitment also prods us to see that, by virtue of its healthy African American citizens, our Beloved Community—the just society that we imagine—could only really be an America that has been radically transformed. Indeed, the state of African American health would be the meaning and measure of that transformation. This makes perfect sense; after all, the then-and-current state of our health as well as the unrelenting and unspeakable racial disparities in health are outcomes rooted in the persistence of racism and the systems and structures of racial subordination. Our "good bodily health" was and is not what these systems intend or ever intended.

Consequently, our collective achievement of good bodily health will be the result of our having purposefully changed our health practices and our having transformed the systems and practices in our society that harm our health—including harms caused by "ingesting" such "items" as pollution dumped in our waterways or released into the atmosphere, or the toxins from waste intentionally sited in and around our communities. It is from these changes that we will erect the Beloved Community, a new society in which our health and wholeness not only matter, but are regarded as part of that society's sacred calling.

A Free People

Though the radically transformative potential of the ninth commitment was probably not something that the Birmingham organizers had in mind when they asked volunteers to "strive to be in good . . . bodily health," the commitment was nevertheless an important aspiration for organizers to have included in the pledge. It communicated to volunteers that care for the body was an integral component of nonviolence, both as a strategy and a way of life. It further conveyed the idea that if volunteers were to dismantle segregation, that victory would be achieved in part by their efforts to achieve good bodily health. Given the day-to-day violence that African Americans faced generally and in the context of the campaign, as well as the general disregard that we experienced over our health and well-being, these important messages were certainly radical enough.

We all, however, can realize the ninth commitment's more far-reaching message, and in this way finish what the campaign started. Thus, as we pursue nonviolence as a way of life, let us do so with the intention to claim good bodily health not only as our birthright, but also as an expression of ourselves as a free people.

6 Cultivate Hope

> *In a time of war, genocide, ecological disasters, and xenophobia, the need for a worldview that anchors daily life to the calling of hope and transformation is undeniable.*
>
> **—Melissa Santosa**[1]

Disdain for the Promise of Hope

> *The paddy wagon was an experience. I can't deny that. But when we got inside the jail, they did things to us that I didn't imagine they would do. And I think the most shocking part for me is that these were men in authority. These were city officials. If the city officials were doing this to us, then what recourse did we have? That's what I remember going through my mind. If the city commissioner, if the police chief, if Bull Connor is here on their side, then what side do we have? All bets are off.*
>
> **—James W. Stewart**[2]

When I view the photographs and film footage of the 1963 Birmingham Campaign (and many of the other civil rights demonstrations), I am struck immediately, as are many people, by the bravery of the volunteers as they faced down violent mobs, firemen, club-wielding police officers, and attack dogs. But it is not just their bravery that grabs my attention; it is the palpable and unshakable hope—unabashedly expressed by volunteers under circumstances where hope seems, at best, the product of dangerous delusion—that America could, and indeed *would*, be a place where all citizens, without exception, enjoy the promise of liberty, equality, and justice. Through their songs and prayers, through their very postures, volunteers radiated an unconquerable hope, a faith in things not yet seen (to paraphrase Hebrews 11:1).

That is not all I witness. I am equally, viscerally struck by the pure hatred in the faces, words, and conduct of Birmingham's protesting white citizens. Of course, it is not just the violence that assails me; it is also the unmistakable contempt "with which the promise of hope" was being "treated by those in power," as Allan Aubrey Boesak says.[3]

Let me take this a step further. It's clear to me when I look at the photos and film that those who threw rocks and fired water hoses and spat on demonstrators and shoved children into paddy wagons were making abundantly clear that they intended to *kill* hope, to render unimaginable and thus unattainable a different and just order of things for the campaign volunteers, for the African American community in general, and for movement allies.

And they weren't alone.

Those white citizens who stayed home because they quietly disagreed with the violence of their neighbors and friends also intended to kill hope through their continued embrace and support of segregation and racial subordination. So, too, did those who—under the pretense of offering their sympathy for campaign demands—counseled African Americans to take it slow and to be patient, and thus to endure racial subordination just a little longer. ("There comes a time when the cup of endurance runs over," wrote King in his "Letter from a Birmingham City Jail," and "men are no longer willing to be plunged into an abyss of injustice where they experience the blackness of corroding despair.")[4]

However expressed (whether violent or benign), the message that these men, women, and children offered to African Americans was clear: *This* is the reality you must live with. It is the best that you, your children, and your grandchildren can expect. "Segregation now, segregation tomorrow, segregation forever."[5]

Until the universe goes dark.

Our twenty-first-century moment is itself marked by the relentless and shameless disdain with which many of those in power regard "the promise of hope." Although one could argue that such disdain never dissipated, that it congealed in the form of public policies and court decisions adopted during the Reagan years and beyond, it is nevertheless true that those in power have used Barack Obama's election to express their contempt more forthrightly and vociferously.

We hear that disdain in their resistance to any efforts to narrow the widening gap between rich and poor; their refusal to admit the reality of discrimination and inequality, here and abroad; and their rejection of policies that would enable us to address, finally, our dramatic and frightening alteration of the climate. We see this disdain in mean-spirited, class-, gender- and race-based obstructionism in Congress; in our Supreme Court's reversal of some parts of voting rights (while the Court consolidates the ability of corporations potentially to affect elections and grants corporations status beyond that of personhood); in the continued travesty of indefinite detentions and force-feeding at Guantánamo Bay prison; in the relentless fight to prevent universal access to health care; and in the incessant calls for military intervention, everywhere and forever. We recognize that disdain in the nostalgia for slavery and for a vision of the 1950s that fails to take into account rigid gender roles, homophobia, and the subjugation of African Americans. We register that disdain in the criminalization of the poor and in the scapegoating of immigrants. (As I write, protestors expressing decidedly xenophobic rhetoric have gathered at our borders to prevent the government from housing and providing care for children who have fled their homes in Central America to escape unimaginable violence.) We note that disdain in the shameless denigration of women on the airwaves and in meetings of state assemblies.

And with the proliferation of social media, talk radio, cable channels, Internet websites, and blogs, we are absolutely bombarded by that disdain. Cynics who speak for, or in the interests of, those in power, who counsel pessimism and despair, who insist on the permanence of what is, seem to be on a continuous, twenty-four-hour loop. Unfortunately, some of us just can't get enough of it. We tune into despair, mire ourselves in it, and often willingly cultivate our own in response.

Killing Hope

> *In Birmingham you would be living in a community where the white man's long-lived tyranny had cowed your people, led them to abandon hope, and developed in them a false sense of inferiority.*
>
> **—Martin Luther King Jr.**[6]

When we succumb to despair, we no longer dream. We learn to accept the idea that we have no agency, no power, no capacity to create a better life for ourselves and others. We look upon the world not with joy, but with sorrow, for we come to believe that the terrible circumstances of our lives are permanent. From this place of hopelessness, we might also come to believe that the larger issues that the world faces—injustice, war, poverty, climate change—are ones that we are powerless to prevent. No longer believing in our own possibilities, we stop working for the benefit of all sentient beings and accept as fruitless any effort to create a more just and peaceful world. In other words, we settle for what is. If we are particularly despairing, we might even accept that we deserve our suffering and thus conclude that we have nothing to live for, nothing to give to others.

"The black experience in America," wrote Charles Johnson, "begins with suffering"—the suffering of capture by African traders, the suffering of the Middle Passage, the suffering of slavery, the suffering of Jim Crow (both the old and the new).[7] It begins, in other words, with our suffering under systems the very essence of which constituted an unspeakable disdain not merely for hope, but for humanity itself. For many of us, our suffering included (and includes) moments of deep and sometimes lasting despair, a sense that we would never be free from violence, hatred, and oppression.

Frederick Douglass captured this despair well when he recalled the decision of his former owner, Thomas Auld, to send him to Edward Covey in order "to be broken." Edward Covey, according to Douglass, "had acquired a very high reputation for breaking young slaves."[8] Douglass wrote,

> If at any one time in my life more than another, I was made to drink the bitterest dregs of slavery, that time was during the first six months of my stay with Mr. Covey. We were worked in all weathers. It was never too hot or too cold; it could never rain, blow, hail, or snow, too hard for us to work in the field. Work, work, work, was scarcely more the order of the day than of the night. The longest days were too short for him, and the shortest nights too long for him. I was somewhat unmanageable when I first went there, but a few months of this discipline tamed me. Mr. Covey succeeded in breaking me. I was broken in body, soul, and spirit. My natural elasticity was crushed, my intellect languished, the disposition to read departed, the cheerful spark that

> lingered about my eye died; the dark night of slavery closed in upon me; and behold a man transformed into a brute![9]

Prior to this experience, Douglass had harbored the hope that he would one day escape to the North, to freedom. With Mr. Covey, however, his faith was almost completely crushed. As Douglass elaborated, "Sunday was my only leisure time. I spent this in a sort of beastlike stupor, between sleep and wake, under some large tree. At times I would rise up, a flash of energetic freedom would dart through my soul, accompanied with a faint beam of hope, that flickered for a moment, and then vanished. I sank down again, mourning over my wretched condition. I was sometimes prompted to take my life, and that of Covey, but was prevented by a combination of hope and fear."[10]

Jim Crow produced similar moments of despair for many African Americans living in the South. Under the tyranny of disenfranchisement, terrorism, segregation, economic exploitation, and myriad acts of state-sponsored and state-sanctioned violence, many African Americans lived and labored without hope that things would change for them or for their progeny. This was true for some Birmingham residents, whose sense of hopelessness under Jim Crow proved too profound for them to support the 1963 campaign, let alone participate in it. Volunteer James Roberson recalled, for example, that during the campaign "there were some ministers that did not partake of any of this, so their churches were never available for the mass meeting. [It] was a radical move to go against segregation and take a stand. Some of us became prisoners within our own mentality—that this is the way it's supposed to be."[11]

When we think about the suffering that is hopelessness, we can easily see that those who treat with disdain communities' aspirations for freedom from hate, violence, and hunger or who insist (however creatively and subtly) that one who is denied rights or brutalized by poverty should neither wish nor dream for anything more, commit what can be rightly characterized as spiritual violence—or, to use Patricia J. Williams's term, "spirit murder." Through their words and their acts, they demonstrate "disregard for others whose lives qualitatively depend on our regard,"[12] as they also reveal their willingness, if not their eagerness, to launch "assaults on the human spirit," to do violence to another's "identity and integrity."[13]

Violence, in fact, "is done whenever we violate" and cut to the core of another person's integrity (as Parker J. Palmer argues); in the realm of politics, we "do violence . . . when we demonize the opposition or ignore human needs in favor of politically expedient decisions."[14] Racism, sexism, "cultural obliteration, prostitution, abandonment of the elderly and homeless, and genocide"—are but a few examples of spiritual violence writ large, according to Williams.[15] And, continues Palmer, "just as physical violence may lead to bodily death, spiritual violence causes death in other guises—the death of a sense of self, of trust in others, of risk taking on behalf of creativity, of commitment to the common good."[16]

In Douglass's case, the system intended to murder his spirit to the maximal extent and reduce human beings to "brutes," to deny that they even had a self, identity, or any integrity. He was also subject to a man whose value to the community was precisely his ability to do violence to the spirit, that is, to kill any "flash of energetic freedom" that would "dart through" an enslaved person's soul. (Tune into talk radio and you will invariably stumble upon a person whose value to the community is that person's willingness to assault "the human spirit" and to incite others to follow suit.)

Ironically and sadly enough, those of us who suffer the peculiar kind of death that results from spirit murder often ourselves become purveyors of despair and cynicism. In the process, we betray our ancestors who held great hopes for us, and poison our families, our relationships, and our communities. Moreover, we create misery that might very well be our sole legacy to future generations, who must then find the wherewithal to heal the harm that we have passed on. In our despair, we might act with complete lack of self-regard. Just as tragically, when we feel as if we have nothing to hope for, no good to claim as our birthright, we can become hateful and even violent toward others.

We, too, can become killers of hope.

The Hopes of the Powerful

> *No matter who is in power, do those in power serve justice, dignity, and humanity? Do they bring hope to the hopeless?*
>
> —**Allan Aubrey Boesak**[17]

The killing of hope by some within the African American

community was true, unfortunately, during the course of the Birmingham Campaign. Although many certainly cheered on the demonstrators and provided quiet moral support (even if they did not actively participate in the movement), others stood on the sidelines, announcing their belief that all was hopeless, and counseling demonstrators and allies alike to accept that nothing good would come of their efforts. "My husband didn't ever go [to the protests]," Emma Smith Young recounted as she discussed her and her children's involvement in the campaign. "He didn't pay any attention to the movement. He thought nothing of it. He said, 'Them folk going to kill y'all out there acting a fool.' That's all he would tell us."[18] Having been cowed, apparently, by "the white man's long-lived tyranny," Young's husband abandoned hope and, in turn, sought to kill with cynicism and despair the hope that stirred his family to put their lives on the line for freedom.

As this example so aptly illustrates, cynicism (as Boesak puts it) "makes us believers only of 'what we see,' that which can be conjured up by the powers of domination, held up us [*sic*] eternal, self-evident truths. It makes us believers in the myths on which those powers depend."[19] When we embrace cynicism, we come to believe "that we are helpless, that evil is unstoppable and irreversible, that there is nothing we can do."[20] For these reasons, cynicism and despair serve systems of subordination, transforming us into the very instruments by which the violence of these systems is maintained.

It should come as no surprise, therefore, that many who are in positions of power cultivate cynicism at every turn, characterizing change as unrealistic and naïve, as the dreams of people who live in a world of fantasy. How often have we heard from corporate executives, government officials, and others, for example, that we cannot realistically hold accountable for the mortgage crisis and resulting economic meltdown of 2008 the financial institutions and their CEOs because they are "too big to fail" (as if the rest of us are too small to care for or to regard)? Underlying their claim is their expectation that we will see the light, i.e., we will accept the fact that our calls for justice and accountability are hopelessly naïve, if not completely disconnected from reality.

Or how about those politicians who shift conversations about the need to eliminate poverty to discussions about the presumed criminality, deficiencies, and immorality of the poor? When politicians do this, they are telling us that it is unrealistic to eradicate poverty because the poor, in their view, deserve their plight. Consequently, our belief that the poor need not "always" be "with us" (to paraphrase Matthew 26:11) is, these politicians tell us, the epitome of naïveté—in spite of evidence to the contrary that we clearly have the resources to make poverty a thing of the past, and have had those resources for quite some time.

Though overwhelming evidence shows that we have dramatically changed our climate, many powerful actors—from corporate boardrooms to Senate chambers to neighborhood religious institutions—insist otherwise, claiming that those of us who accept the evidence are gullible, that our proposals to address climate change cannot trump corporate needs, and that in any case it is too late for us to tackle the issue (so why bother?).

Then, of course, are the endless ways in which those who benefit from and are invested in the persistence of racism counsel us to *just stop talking about it*. On the one hand, they tell us that our refusal to accept racism as anything other than a permanent feature of everyday life is our failure to accept reality. On the other, they claim that we actually *cause* racism when we insist that it be addressed structurally. "In my colleagues' view," Justice Sonia Sotomayor notes, in her dissent from the Court's racism-blind *Schuette v. BAMN* decision, "examining the racial impact of legislation only perpetuates racial discrimination. This refusal to accept the stark reality that race matters is regrettable. The way to stop discrimination on the basis of race is to speak openly and candidly on the subject of race, and to apply the Constitution with eyes open to the unfortunate effects of centuries of racial discrimination."[21]

Understandably, some of us have embraced these claims about what is realistic, "cowed" by those in power. Others of us have cynically embraced such master narratives because we have discovered ways to profit personally from them. However we look at it, though, we cannot escape the fact that despair and cynicism are "the language" of empire's dreams *for* us.[22] Thus, when we ourselves speak from that language, we not only treat hope with disdain but align our interests, and consequently become one, with those in power.

Hope and Nonviolence

> *When they started marching, I saw them turn the water hose on Carlton Reese and knock him as high up as a field is long. When he came back down, he hit the ground singing, "I ain't gonna let nobody turn me around. I'm gonna keep on walking, I'm gonna keep on talking, marching up to freedom land."*
>
> **—Eva Lou Billingsley Russell**[23]

If despair and cynicism are the language of empire's dreams for us, then hope—as Boesak so persuasively argues—must ultimately be a powerful form of resistance and the stuff with which we dismantle systems of subordination and build a more just world. Indeed, hope proclaims that there is absolutely "nothing naïve about justice, dignity, and equality and the struggle for a better world" and thus nothing permanent about subordination or empire.[24] It unmasks realism's appropriation by those in power, the fictions upon which they proclaim their rightness, justness, and invincibility.

But let's go a step further. View once again the footage and photographs of the Birmingham protests. Look closely at the counter-demonstrators, the police, the firemen. Yes, we can see the disdain with which they treated the promise of hope. But we can also see this: that hope is a powerful, destabilizing, and radical force that threatens the status quo. After all, it causes one to get up singing even after one has been knocked to the ground by the forces of hate and violence. As Henry M. Goodgame

Sr. explains about his participation in the Birmingham demonstrations, "You had that fear that something was going to happen, but you still had something else beside that fear that pushed you forward. It overrode fear and the inferiority complex. It was that drive that you had to express yourself. You said to yourself, 'I don't like it, and I want to do something about it.' And so you get at those marches. Yes, you're afraid, but you still had that drive. You still had that incentive to go on in spite of what might happen."[25]

We should never take lightly the power of hope.

As should be clear by now, hope is also the lifeblood of nonviolence (as the Birmingham images also reveal to us), for nonviolence presupposes that we can successfully establish love as the basis of our conduct, as well as of our relations with one another, with other sentient beings, and with Earth itself. Furthermore, nonviolence is an expression of faith in the capacity of our so-called enemy to touch his or her own humanity and, as a result, recognize and honor ours. It is fundamentally an optimistic philosophy; in the face of oppression, nonviolence counsels neither hate nor despair and thus speaks an eloquent counter-narrative to the story that those in power tell us and themselves—ultimately to their own detriment, spiritual and otherwise—in order to rationalize the unjust order of things.

Because hope is the lifeblood of nonviolence, nonviolence transforms your relationship to, and investment in, the way things are. No longer constrained by the fictions reified by those in power, you live—you *demonstrate*—a radical realism, as Boesak writes, which "the realism of politics cannot abide."[26]

This radical realism, the stuff of hope, is not to be mistaken for a fantasy world to which we turn when we do not want to face difficult issues. Nor is it the realism offered by politicians who invariably define our yearnings for justice and peace in ways that support the status quo. Instead, this realism, this hope, is both a critique that demystifies power and an instrument through which we rescue justice from the realm of the impossible.

We should be clear: such hope is powerful and real only if it is lived, only if it is transformed into a practice that we hone until hope fills the very core of our being, expressing itself through all we say and do. To make hope this kind of practice, then, let us once again turn to the Birmingham Campaign.

Hope Is a Practice

> *Hope is a verb; hope is something you do. When you practice hope, you bring hope into the world of human events. The more we practice hope the better we get at it.*
>
> **—Joe Volk**[27]

Although I have already discussed the first Birmingham Campaign commitment (Meditate daily on the teachings and life of Jesus), what I did not say about it is that it also offers—perhaps more clearly than the other commitments—a practice of hope. It could be read, for instance, as a commandment that implicitly challenged volunteers to cultivate hope by claiming as their own the meaning of Jesus' death and resurrection, which is that he triumphed over state-sponsored injustice and violence (or, as Boesak argues about the resurrection, over the "power of violence").[28] Like Jesus, volunteers, too, would defeat state-sponsored violence (racial segregation), and in so doing usher in a new society, one grounded in reconciliation and friendship.

By meditating on the teachings and life of Jesus, then, volunteers would have been immersing themselves in a worldview from which they could have written their own counter-narrative of hope and transformation, a story that segregationists would not have been able to entomb within their narrative of a permanent order of white supremacy—within, that is, their politics of realism and (for African Americans) despair.

Taking a cue once again, then, from the Birmingham Campaign's first commitment, we pledge to practice and cultivate hope. We can start in the way that the campaign card suggests: by actively seeking out and immersing ourselves in the works of wisdom-teachers who remind us of our strength, vision, and purpose. This literature might very well include the teachings of Jesus, but there is no reason we should not expand our repertoire to include others who inspire and motivate us—from Arundhati Roy to Michael Bernard Beckwith, from Chögyam Trungpa Rinpoche to Audre Lorde.

We adopt this practice not only because our wisdom-teachers remind us of our best selves, but also because they remind us that we belong to each other, a truth that we too easily forget in difficult times. So much of the hatred and violence that we suffer is a consequence of our misremembering ourselves in the other, of misremembering that every single one of us—*including* those in power who treat hope with disdain—

wants to be safe, free from harm, and not to suffer. Through our teachers' promptings, we recall our own wisdom and, with that, our capacity to be love and to do justice.

When we contemplate "the difficult days ahead,"[29] (as King put it)—that is, the challenges of cutting through materialism, greed, hatred, violence, enmity, and despair in order to realize a world grounded not simply in peace, but nonviolence—our teachers remind us that power comes from our fearless embrace of hope, against all odds and against all efforts to destroy it.

This practice actually takes you right back to the Fifth Mindfulness Training, for in many respects you are moved to scrutinize whether or not you have been consuming what nurtures your faith in a hopeful vision of society. Are you on a steady diet of items seeped in cynicism and despair, which you then share with others? If so, what affect does this diet have on your capacity to dream, on your willingness to step into the fray, and on your hopes for your family and community? To what degree have you become, as a result of your diet, resigned to the reality of racism, economic injustice, endless war, and poverty?

Although the toxicity of much of what is available to us for our consumption is usually quite obvious, sometimes the items we consume (books, radio programs, articles, to name a few), because we agree with the authors' point of view and because they are salient critiques of the status quo, also promote pessimism and even express a subtle disdain for hope.

Yet as Peter Gabel has argued, a "successful critical approach to the present requires the illumination of the injustice of what is, *anchored in a transcendent intuition of the just world that ought to be.*"[30] Therefore, whereas we ourselves—and our analyses—might well be "anchored in a transcendent intuition of the just world that ought to be," we sometimes fail to honor that by speaking truth explicitly and unabashedly from that place—often because we are afraid that we would not be taken seriously, or because we equate the aspirational with either a lack of political rigor or with critical vacuity or irrationality. Perhaps on some level we simply do not believe that we could make that "just world" possible. We fail, in fact, for a host of reasons, many of which are unquestionably legitimate but that nevertheless bring us to the same uninspiring and uninspired place. At some point, however, it would behoove us to ask just whom this failure of hope ultimately serves.

At any rate, we can cultivate hope by developing the daily practice of reading works that both inspire and critique, that encourage us to be rigorous in how we frame the just world that we envision and hopeful about our capacity to bring that world into being. We can expand our practices of hope by also cultivating speech that inspires hope. The Fourth Mindfulness Training actually provides great guidance in this regard, and is itself a worthy pledge to make. It reads:

> *Aware of the suffering caused by unmindful speech and the inability to listen to others, I am committed to cultivating loving speech and deep listening in order to bring joy and happiness to others and relieve others of their suffering. Knowing that words can create happiness or suffering, I am determined to speak truthfully, with*

words that inspire self-confidence, joy, and hope. I will not spread news that I do not know to be certain and will not criticize or condemn things of which I am not sure. I will refrain from uttering words that cause division or discord, or that can cause the family or community to break. I am determined to make all efforts to reconcile and resolve all conflicts, however small.[31]

Those who seek to kill hope often use as their weapon speech filled with untruths, cynicism, misinformation, discord, closed-mindedness, and condemnation. We defuse this weapon with a refusal to speak in unmindful ways: i.e., with the willingness to exercise circumspection and thoughtfulness about what we say so that when we speak, we speak what is true as well as what creates community and peace—even when the truth is difficult to bear because it demands radical change on everyone's part.

Use the Fourth Mindfulness Training, therefore, as you would the Fifth—to look deeply into your life and how you conduct yourself. Are your conversations immersed in negativity, conflict, and disparagement? When you engage others, do you listen, inspire hope, speak truthfully, and create community? Do you speak when it is actually better not to speak at all?

Another way we can cultivate hope is by actively participating in a community of folk who, as a matter of principle, refuse to engage in the politics of despair. When we choose to surround ourselves with naysayers, we can start to feel as if we are justified in a bleak view of the world and of others outside of our community, as well as the belief that those who counsel hope are foolish and so unworthy of serious consideration. Just as damaging, the negative community might enable us to make peace with suffering and withdraw into a world cut off from any real concern for others.

Do you belong to such a community, and are you one of its enablers? Do you reinforce cynicism and hopelessness? If so, what effect has this negativity had on your view of others, on your capacity to dream, on your willingness to become actively involved in change? What is required of you to help transform this community into one that hopes and dreams?

These and other practices are vital means for us to nurture and sustain hope, to live it on a day-to-day basis, and thereby embody an alternative to the cynicism to which we are regularly subjected. Yet, these practices are not enough in and of themselves, for in the final analysis it is only through our pursuit of a just society that we are able not only to touch and experience the full power of hope but of our own power as well.

Hope and the Shape of a Just World

In 1963, as a teenager, I had the good fortune of participating in the "Birmingham Campaign" for civil rights led by Reverend King. It was a hopeful time. Feeling part of a larger community of like-minded nonviolent protestors, I felt buoyed up by the possibility of triumph over injustice. When,

> *later, after leaders like Malcolm X, King, and the Kennedys had been struck down by violence, a period of hopelessness settled in.*
>
> *For many of us today that hopelessness still seems to hold sway. And so, before we endeavor to change the world, we need to rekindle hope again. The thing I've learned about hope, however, is that it grows from action, not from thought. If we wish to see an enlightened world of peace and justice for all, we have to move beyond merely imagining it, to nonviolent actions, however small, that will help to usher it in.*
>
> **—Jan Willis**[32]

When we adopt nonviolence as a way of life, we make hope the language that we speak, the way we move in the world, and the basis of our political action. Nonviolence, however, compels us to ground our practices of hope in our active commitment to transform the world—and to transform it specifically *from the bottom up*. Nonviolence directs us to the bottom because "the shape of a just world," as Boesak rightly argues, "lies in the fulfillment of the hopes of the poor and powerless, the silenced and the downtrodden, not the elites whose wealth has flourished beyond their wildest dreams, even as they trample on the dreams of the poor."[33]

Practices of hope that do not move us to see and pursue justice and peace, from the point of view of those who bear the full brunt of the violence in our society, are practices that protect solely the interests of those in power, and, as a consequence, leave intact systems of subordination. They leave untouched, in other words, the very structures that our commitment to nonviolence requires us to transform.

Thus, hope should not leave us in a comfortable place. Instead, it should make us tremble. For hope—if it is authentic—forces us to face (and find the capacity to do so with grace, faith, and love) both the enormity of the challenge before us *and* just how deeply implicated and entangled are our own hopes in the current order of things. As Boesak explains, hope "challenges and confronts us before it inspires us."[34] If we are not shaken to our roots, then what we call "hope" might in fact be a cover for our unattended despair and a sign of our quiet surrender to what is.

This truth about hope is poignantly illustrated by the Birmingham Campaign volunteers. Their hope drove them to the battle lines, where they not only encountered hate, violence, and the possibility of death, but also (we can imagine) any inclination that they might have had to acquiesce to, and thus leave undisturbed, the status quo. Conversely, the battle lines were the places where volunteers fortified their hope, where they held it for themselves and discovered that *they could hold it as well for those in power* who sought to crush hope outright and obliterate volunteers' will to dream and to be free. It was at the battle lines, finally, where the volunteers truly touched and experienced the awesome power of hope, where they discovered that they would not, indeed, "let nobody turn" them " 'round."

These lines of conflict where power weighs in most heavily—"the difficult strife-torn places where bruised, wounded, and dejected people struggle for meaningful life and in that struggle find hope," to quote Boesak[35]—are where hope takes us. We commit to the practice of hope with full awareness not only that these places are where we must confront power, but that confronting power where it is most fiercely exercised is precisely the bargain we make with ourselves when we choose to pledge our lives to nonviolence. But we make *this* bargain as well: that at these battle lines we will hold hope not only for ourselves, but also for those who treat with disdain the promise of hope—the powerful as well as those "cowed" by tyranny. It is a practice that nonviolence calls for, and it is a practice to which we unhesitatingly pledge our lives.

#conclusion

The Kalamas who were inhabitants of Kesaputta sitting on one side said to the Blessed One: "There are some monks and brahmans, venerable sir, who visit Kesaputta. They expound and explain only their own doctrines; the doctrines of others they despise, revile, and pull to pieces. Some other monks and brahmans too, venerable sir, come to Kesaputta. They also expound and explain only their own doctrines; the doctrines of others they despise, revile, and pull to pieces. Venerable sir, there is doubt, there is uncertainty in us concerning them. Which of these reverend monks and brahmans spoke the truth and which falsehood?"

"It is proper for you, Kalamas, to doubt, to be uncertain; uncertainty has arisen in you about what is doubtful. Come, Kalamas. Do not go upon what has been acquired by repeated hearing; nor upon tradition; nor upon rumor; nor upon what is in a scripture; nor upon surmise; nor upon an axiom; nor upon specious reasoning; nor upon a bias towards a notion that has been pondered over; nor upon another's seeming ability; nor upon the consideration, 'The monk is our teacher.' Kalamas, when you yourselves know: 'These things are bad; these things

are blamable; these things are censured by the wise; undertaken and observed, these things lead to harm and ill,' abandon them."

—The Instruction to the Kalamas[1]

On Violence

I don't see how any revolution—I've never heard of a non-violent revolution or a revolution that was brought about by turning the other cheek, and so I believe that it is a crime for anyone to teach a person who is being brutalized to continue to accept that brutality without doing something to defend himself. If this is what the Christian-Gandhian philosophy teaches then it is criminal—a criminal philosophy.

—Malcolm X[2]

Doubt, incredulousness, disbelief, repudiation—these are just some of the responses that many of us have offered (and continue to offer) to the challenge of nonviolence. What about the hard-heartedness of our "enemies"? Why should we be nonviolent when they are more than willing to protect their interests at all costs—even if that means slaughtering the peaceful? Hasn't history proved that, on the whole, only violence (or the threat thereof) changes things and that nonviolence ultimately does not work?

Having witnessed and experienced the violence that whites often perpetrated with impunity against African Americans, both on an everyday basis and specifically during the civil rights movement, many African Americans, by the mid-1960s, came to these conclusions and therefore did not buy into nonviolence as a viable or ultimately effective means to secure freedoms and our peace. Moreover, for many during that time it seemed that the arc of the universe was bending inexorably toward armed revolutionary struggle—as the victories over colonial rule in Africa, Asia, and other parts of the world clearly demonstrated.

We reasoned, for example, that it wasn't nonviolence that persuaded France to get out of Vietnam and Algeria or the English to give up Kenya. Nonviolence did not secure the liberation of the Cuban masses from Batista's rule. No, these revolutions demonstrated that the only thing that worked, and the only thing that would work, is violence. "All of the third world political movements that are forcing the retreat of colonialism have learned to deal with the expeditionary armies of colonialism," observed George Jackson. "There is no case of successful liberation without violence. How could you neutralize an army without violence?"[3]

To a great extent, such assessments of violence and nonviolence, set against both the continued violence and intransigence of whites on the issue of black freedom and the successes of decolonization, were the valuations from which the Black Power Movement evolved, as they were also the impetus for the creation of organizations such as the Black Panther Party for Self-Defense (BPP). Party founder Huey P. Newton himself noted that "we had seen Martin Luther King come to Watts in an effort to calm the people, and we had seen his philosophy of nonviolence rejected. Black people had been taught nonviolence;

it was deep in us. What good, however, was nonviolence when the police were determined to rule by force? . . . Everything we had seen convinced us that our time had come. Out of this need sprang the Black Panther Party."[4] Evoking in its Ten Point Platform and Program both the Second Amendment right to bear arms and the right, as expressed in the Declaration of Independence, "to throw off" a government that "evinces a design to reduce [the people] under absolute despotism," the Black Panther Party embraced as a viable option armed self-defense and revolution as a means to secure the liberation of the nation's "black colonial subjects." The BPP's message unquestionably resonated with many African Americans, and they increasingly viewed appeals to nonviolence as out of touch with the realities and trajectory of black aspirations here and abroad.

Of course, even at the height of the Birmingham Campaign some were skeptical about nonviolence, in practice and belief, even as they supported the campaign itself. "My father and several other men in the neighborhood set up night patrols," recalled volunteer Annetta Streeter Gary. "My daddy did not believe in weapons. I know that he was not armed, but I know that some were, because everyone did not believe in nonviolence."[5] Indeed, this became painfully clear when, after the May 11, 1963, bombing of Birmingham's A. G. Gatson Hotel and the home of Reverend A. D. King, the African American community responded by burning buildings, overturning cars, and engaging in other protest activities that were the antithesis of nonviolent civil disobedience. Ultimately, federal troops were brought into Birmingham to quell the unrest.

Nonviolence was not the answer, for everyone, to white violence and injustice or the means to secure black freedom.

To Know for Yourself

> *When Dr. King invoked "the Beloved Community" as an ideal, I thought he meant something simple-minded like the Bad Guys Stop the Bad Stuff and the Good Guys Then Forgive Them—for the sake of an okay existence. It took me a while to get past the "we" versus "they" way of looking at things. It took me a long time, absolutely, before I understood that "Beloved Community" means everybody is sacred. Nobody is excluded from that deliberate embrace.*
>
> **—June Jordan**[6]

I was raised on Black Power discourse and politics. I also believe there is great truth in many of the analyses offered by those who repudiated nonviolence. (On the issue of revolutions in Africa and elsewhere, however, critics never really addressed whether these revolutions were organized and purposeful nonviolent struggles in the first instance—South Africa excepted.) Indeed, over the course of most of my life I believed more in Malcolm X's "by any means necessary" than in "only a refusal to hate or kill can put an end to the chain of violence in the world."[7]

Yet it had never occurred to me—not once—actually *to try* nonviolence for myself, to test it out, that is, *as a way of life* (although over the years I have certainly engaged in a number of nonviolent direct actions and have even undertaken civil disobedience trainings). In fact, if anyone had suggested to me that I embark on such a journey, I would have laughed outright—and then I would have damned nonviolence from what I had "acquired by repeated hearing," "rumor," and "the doctrines of others." I certainly would not have dismissed such an approach from my own lived experience of nonviolence and thus from my own test of the very "doctrines" to which I so rigidly adhered (I imagine this was true for most who rejected nonviolence during the civil rights movement, and I imagine this is true for many people today).

I would like to suggest that embracing nonviolence as a way of life allows us to see another way to think about the so-called effectiveness and ineffectiveness or victories and failures of both violence and nonviolence. Indeed, as I have embarked upon this journey I have come to realize that because I had not tried nonviolence for myself as a way of life, I missed entirely this crucial truth: nonviolence *works*, and it works the very moment that you live and breathe it, and make it the very basis of how you treat yourself and engage with others. It works because in such moments as these you have transformed your own relationship to violence such that it no longer claims you as either its victim or its collaborator. Therefore, even if one's nonviolent tactics "fail"—and they often will[8]—one's lived commitment to nonviolence is always already a victory not only for you, but for everyone, because you are one less person in the world who does violence and justifies it in the name of peace or justice or even love. You are one less person, in other words, in whom violence is able to take up residence.

Permit me to go even further. I am willing to bet that we have yet to realize the full power of nonviolence as a method by which to create meaningful change—even to overcome tyranny itself—because most of us have not, by and large, practiced it from a place of deep surrender, from our full embrace of the creed. In fact, we should consider the possibility that any lingering or unacknowledged attachments that we have to violence—however slight—actually stifle our political imaginations and thus limit our strategies from the start.

I also missed another crucial insight when I failed to discover for myself what is true: Violence works in exactly the same way. That is to say, it also works the moment that you allow yourself to become it and to engage with the world accordingly.

Therefore, an important question, it seems to me, is not merely whether violence or nonviolence is more effective in bringing about meaningful change; it is whether or not we want *to be* violence, even if just for a moment, and whether or not we want what that moment creates for us and for others, which is, in truth, more violence. After all, as Barry L. Gan has noted, our "use of violence *guarantees* the continuance of violence simply because" we ourselves are "using it."[9] Thus, violence creates exactly what it intends. Moreover, it will reside in whatever "peace" one achieves, in whatever "justice" one effects, and in whatever institutions one creates or life one carves out in its aftermath.

When any of us champions violence as a solution—as our nation is doing, for example, in the Middle East today—we need to have an honest conversation with ourselves, one in which we wonder: What does it do to those who turn to it as a solution? And what do they create—what kind of society do they manifest—from their embrace of violence? What happens to the violence once the confrontation ends, where does it go, what kind of home does it make, what facade of respectability does it adopt, and just how close beneath the surface does it lie so that we can always easily harness it, yet once again, to impose our interests?

As I say this, I am "painfully aware," to quote Boesak, "that deeply complex situations arise where nonviolent intervention comes too late, where the world, for various reasons, has hesitated too long, has erred fatally on the side of greed, neglect, or indifference, has invested too vastly and for too long in the entrenchment of tyrants of all kinds."[10] There simply will be times when some will hold onto power at all costs and will thus willingly destroy everything in order to keep from having to give up anything. (One need only look at what Bashar al-Assad is today doing to "his" Syria to see how this is getting played out.)

But if it is *really* too late, if the *only* solution to a wretched situation that we have created is for us to meet violence with violence, then we should never do so with anything less than a broken heart. We should show no glee, no sense of righteous retribution, no romanticization of our armed selves, no desire to make holy the violence that we will visit upon others, and thus no assertion that we will, for example, hunt someone "down to the gates of hell."[11] We should make no attempt to construct those whom we will harm as anything less than our brothers and sisters—no matter how unspeakable their conduct. When we—any of us, or any nation in the world—"pick up the gun," we should feel absolutely nothing but immense sorrow.

Perhaps the more important question, therefore, isn't whether or not nonviolence or violence works; instead, it is whether or not by our investments in tyranny, our hesitation to speak up and act against injustice, our "greed, neglect, or indifference," we have ultimately *failed nonviolence itself.*

You don't have to take my word for any of this, of course. But at least try nonviolence so that, in the Buddha's words, "you yourselves know: 'These things are bad; these things are blamable: these things are censured by the wise; undertaken and observed, these things lead to harm and ill,' abandon them." True, you might discover that nonviolence does not work. But you might also find, as I have, that nonviolence will move you to be a force for change in the world.

We Are the Ones

When Martin Luther King Jr. decided in 1967 that it was time to break his silence about the U.S. war in Vietnam, he offered the following as one of the reasons why he finally chose to speak out:

> As I have walked among the desperate, rejected and angry young men I have told them that Molotov cocktails and rifles would not solve their problems. I have tried to offer them my deepest compassion while maintaining my conviction that social change comes most meaningfully through nonviolent

> action. But they asked—and rightly so—what about Vietnam? They asked if our own nation wasn't using massive doses of violence to solve its problems, to bring about the changes it wanted. Their question hit home, and I knew that I could never again raise my voice against the violence of the oppressed in the ghettos without having first spoken clearly to the greatest purveyor of violence in the world today—my own government.[12]

We are not the only ones tasked with meeting the challenge of nonviolence. So also is our government, from the women and men who serve on our police forces to those who serve as our representatives in state houses, in Congress, and in the White House. Too often, and in our name, they adopt policies and practices that reflect their own investments in violence; too often, they act in ways that render us all purveyors "of violence in the world today." Indeed, we need (and must actively seek) a government that embraces and champions nonviolence as a matter of policy, both domestic and foreign.

So what about Guantánamo Bay prison? It is just as good a place as any to start demanding such a policy change.

As I write this conclusion, the prisoners' hunger strike has surpassed five hundred days. Although they have been subjected to the violence that is forcefeeding—a practice that our government is working tirelessly to prevent from being exposed to the public—and although some have discontinued their strike, a number of prisoners nevertheless remain committed and continue to call attention to the injustice of their detention; to our betrayal of our stated commitment to freedom and democracy; and ultimately to our own moral bankruptcy.

Further, by their disobedience and willingness to engage in self-imposed suffering, they demonstrate in no uncertain terms that Guantánamo Bay ("GITMO") is where nonviolence must take us, where love, compassion, forgiveness, and hope must take us, because it is yet another place where the full brunt of the violence in our society—and of our misguided response to the violence that we have suffered—is brought to bear. When we consider the fact that the indefinite detention of these men is grounded in part in a racial logic that underlies the stateside mass incarceration of black and brown men, it is clear that we are not untouched by the injustice that is GITMO. Indeed, that institution may serve to rationalize the further criminalization of black and brown men throughout our nation.

We therefore cannot sit idly by while this travesty continues. As we meet the challenge of nonviolence issued in Birmingham fifty years ago, we must of necessity turn to our government—our representatives—and demand that it does the same. For let us be clear: GITMO is violence itself. It manifests the brutal exercise of violence on the part of our government and consequently on our part as well.

Since I made my pledge of support for the prisoners, I have written to my representatives in Congress, regularly shared articles and information about the prisoners' plight, and engaged in other activities, including fasting. Having set up a Google Alert for news on the hunger strike, I now receive, on a daily basis, updates on the strike and the response by our government to it. I share this information as often as I can.

I am now even more committed to the closure of GITMO.

As I said in the introduction, the pledge—*and* writing this book—have taken me on a journey, to the challenges that I scarcely anticipated. As I have become more committed to closing Guantánamo Bay prison, I have also become more aware of and in touch with the suffering around me from the everyday violence of hunger, miseducation, xenophobia, drug wars, sexism, poverty. At the same time, I have become more in tune with my own *stuff,* my own internal rages and thoughts of unkindness, my own subtle contributions to the tension in a room, on public transportation, in conversations. I have been astonished to find just how often I imagine myself initiating a violent confrontation over some imagined slight from a complete stranger, how quickly I flip the bird when I drive, and how easily I can be indifferent to the needs of others. Such awareness has forced me to confront what I do, or don't do, on an everyday basis, contributes to an atmosphere that makes Guantánamo possible. In so doing, I have doubled down on many of the practices that I have described here.

My day starts with meditation. I practice courtesy with great intention. I read regularly the works of our wisdom-teachers. And I will laugh at myself—kindly, of course—when I see that I am taking great offense at small things.

Honestly, though, I haven't always been consistent, and this has been true as well for my Guantánamo pledge. Sometimes I forget about the prisoners and their hunger strike; sometimes I forget to fast or I simply decide that I just want to eat because there's nothing easy at all about fasting, even for a brief period of time. In short, I haven't always "kept" my pledge, not by a long shot. I can certainly do more.

And I will because this is, as I've said, a journey, not an endpoint. Moreover, I have learned that once you make the pledge, it is simply impossible to sit *comfortably* with your own complacency and inaction on anything meaningful in your life. *Always* my pledge—this pledge, my Guantánamo pledge—gently reminds me of my better self, of my capacity to give and to serve others. Always it reminds me that, from this place of privilege that I occupy, there is more I can do. But it is not a reminder that is about guilt or shame, however. It is just that saying "yes" to nonviolence changes you—is changing me—absolutely.

Like the Birmingham volunteers, then, I will not give up. I'll keep at it because I must, because it is just, and because that is what nonviolence and my promise to live it compel me to do.

This was the ultimate hope of the Birmingham Campaign: that we African Americans, touched by the power of nonviolence, would embrace it as a way of life and in so doing become a force for change not only for ourselves, but also the world. "Nonviolence, the answer to the Negroes' need," writes King, "may become the answer to the most desperate need of all humanity."[13] By allowing the spirit of nonviolence *to work through us*, in other words, we would make irresistible to all children, women, and men the "sheer morality of its claim" and thus heal a world desperately in need of an ethic of love.

Thus, let us all embrace this legacy of nonviolence with our whole selves, and do so not out of some sense or belief that it is African Americans' particular burden to bear. It is not. But if we are the only ones to step forward, then so be it. Let us be, in the words of June Jordan, "the ones we have been waiting for,"[14] and in so doing, finally manifest our sacred Beloved Community.

#references

Introduction

1. Martin Luther King Jr. "A Case against 'Tokenism'," in *A Testament of Hope: The Essential Writings and Speeches of Martin Luther King Jr.* edited by James M. Washington. San Francisco: Harper, 1986, p. 109.
2. King. *Why We Can't Wait* in Washington, *op. cit.*, p. 536.
3. *Ibid.*
4. "James W. Stewart," in *Foot Soldiers for Democracy: The Men, Women, and Children of the Birmingham Civil Rights Movement* edited by Horace Huntley and John W. McKerley. Chicago and Urbana: University of Illinois Press, 2009, p. 137.
5. King. *Why We Can't Wait* in Washington, *op cit.*, p. 536.
6. *Ibid.*, p. 537.
7. *Ibid.*
8. *Ibid.*
9. S. L. Taudin Chabot. "Crossing the Great Divide: The Gandhian Repertoire's Transnational Diffusion to the American Civil Rights Movement." Ph.D. thesis, 2003, p. 211 <http://dare.uva.nl/document/187124>.
10. "Carrie Delores Hamilton Lock," in Huntley and McKerley, *op. cit.*, p. 202.
11. King. "An Experiment in Love," in Washington, *op. cit.*, p. 17.
12. Martin Luther King, Jr. "The Negro Is Part of that Huge

Community Who Seek New Freedom in Every Area of Life," in *Martin Luther King, Jr. and the Global Freedom Struggle*. From Stanford University, The Martin Luther King, Jr., Research and Education Institute <goo.gl/71XMOy>.

13. *Ibid.*
14. *Ibid.*
15. "Let us realize the arc of the moral universe is long but it bends toward justice." King. "Where Do We Go from Here?", in Washington, *op. cit.*, p. 252.
16. King. "The Power of Nonviolence," in Washington, *op. cit.*, p. 13.
17. His Holiness the Dalai Lama. *Beyond Religion: Ethics for a Whole World*. Boston: Mariner Books, 2012, p. xiii.
18. King. "A Time to Break Silence," in Washington, *op. cit.*, p. 242.
19. King. "Remaining Awake Through a Great Revolution (March 31, 1968)," in Washington, *op. cit.*, p. 276.
20. King. *Why We Can't Wait* in Washington, *op. cit.*, p. 537.
21. "A Hunger for Justice: Guantanamo Day 100,"by Seventh Sister, May 16, 2013 <http://open.salon.com/blog/seventhsister/2013/05/16/a_hunger_for_justice_guantanamo_day_100>.

Chapter 1: Commandments to Live By

1. "Carlton Reese," in *Foot Soldiers for Democracy: The Men, Women, and Children of the Birmingham Civil Rights Movement* edited by Horace Huntley and John W. McKerley. Chicago and Urbana: University of Illinois Press, 2009, p. 101.
2. "Christ furnished the spirit and motivation, while Gandhi furnished the method." Martin Luther King, Jr. "An Experiment in Love," in *A Testament of Hope: The Essential Writings and Speeches of Martin Luther King Jr.* edited by James M. Washington. San Francisco: Harper, 1986, p. 17. Although King wrote this statement five years prior to the Birmingham Campaign and in the context of the Montgomery Bus Boycott, it was nevertheless

a belief that he expressed throughout his career. It was an idea that he most likely conveyed to volunteers when he taught on nonviolence during the Campaign's mass meetings.

3. King. "A Testament of Hope," in Washington, *op. cit.*, p. 328.
4. "Are you willing to commit to following Jesus' example," writes Michael Bernard Beckwith, "and inwardly practice as he did? His state of Christ consciousness was not ready-made; he worked for it through his spiritual practices of meditation, prayer, contemplation, introspection, and solitary retreats. He was Jesus the man who became Jesus the Christ; the same Christ that each of us is when we become self-realized." Beckwith, *Spiritual Liberation: Fulfilling Your Soul's Potential.* New York: Atria, 2008, p. 146.
5. Joseph Goldstein. "Three Means to Peace," in *Mindful Politics: A Buddhist Guide to Making the World a Better Place* edited by Melvin McLeod. Boston: Wisdom, 2006, p. 121.
6. Beckwith, *op cit.*, p. 33. Italics in the original.
7. Bonnie Duran. "Race, Racism and the Dharma," in *Dharma, Color and Culture: New Voices in Western Buddhism* edited by Hilda Gutiérrez Baldoquin. Berkeley: Parallax, 2004, pp. 167–68.
8. Anthony Sampson. *Mandela: The Authorized Biography*. New York: Vintage, 1999, p. 245.
9. King. "Stride toward Freedom," in Washington, *op cit.*, p. 488.
10. Michelle Goldberg. "Yes, Mr. President, the Border Kids Are Refugees," *The Nation*, July 16, 2014.
11. See, for example, Osha Gray Davidson. "Michele Bachmann Salutes the Upside to Slavery," *Forbes*, July 8, 2011; "Cliven Bundy: Are Black People 'Better Off As Slaves' Than 'Under Government Subsidy?' *Huffington Post,* April 24, 2014.
12. Allan Aubrey Boesak. "'Just Another Jew in the Ditch': Incarnated Reconciliation," in *Radical Reconciliation: Beyond Political Pietism and Christian Quietism* by Allan Aubrey Boesak and Curtis Paul DeYoung. Maryknoll: N.Y.: Orbis, 2013, p. 70.

13. *Ibid.*, p. 62.
14. *Ibid.*, p. 69.
15. Desmond Tutu <https://www.goodreads.com/author/quotes/5943.Desmond_Tutu>.
16. King. "Nonviolence and Racial Justice," in Washington, *op. cit.*, p. 8.
17. "LaVerne Revis Martin," in Huntley and McKerley, *op cit.*, p. 91.
18. King. "Letter from a Birmingham City Jail," in Washington, *op cit.*, p. 297.
19. King. "A Time to Break Silence," in Washington, *op cit.*, p. 242.
20. Allan Aubrey Boesak. *Dare We Speak of Hope? Searching for a Language of Life in Faith and Politics*. Grand Rapids: Eerdmans, 2014, p. 115.
21. King. "A Time to Break Silence," in Washington, *op cit.*, p. 242.
22. "Nims E. Gay," in Huntley and McKerley, *op. cit.*, p. 34.
23. "LaVerne Revis Martin," in Huntley and McKerley, *op. cit.*, p. 91.
24. "Carlton Reese," in Huntley and McKerley, *op. cit.*, p. 102.

Chapter 2: Practice Forgiveness

1. Thich Nhat Hanh. "We Are the Continuation of Our Ancestors," Dharma talk given in Plum Village, July 21, 1997 <https://sites.google.com/site/tnhdhamma/Home/test-list/we-are-the-continuation-of-our-ancestors>. The quotes immediately following are from this talk.
2. Martin Luther King Jr. *Strength to Love*. Minneapolis: Fortress, 2010, p. 44.
3. Michele Benzamin-Miki. "To Love Unconditionally Is Freedom," in *Dharma, Color and Culture: New Voices in Western Buddhism* edited by Hilda Gutiérrez Baldoquin. Berkeley: Parallax, 2004, p. 81.
4. Jack Kornfield. *After the Ecstasy, the Laundry*. New York: Bantam, 2000, p. 236.
5. Michael Bernard Beckwith. *Spiritual Liberation: Fulfilling Your Soul's Potential*. New York: Atria, 2008, p. 16.

6. William Still. *The Underground Railroad: Authentic Narratives and First-Hand Accounts* Mineola, New York: Dover, 2007, p. 44.
7. *Ibid.*, pp. 239–41.
8. Audre Lorde. *Sister Outsider*. Trumansburg, N.Y.: Crossing, 1984, p. 127.
9. Allan Aubrey Boesak. "Between Reitz, a Rock, and a Hard Place: Reconciliation after the Reitz Event," in *Radical Reconciliation: Beyond Political Pietism and Christian Quietism* by Allan Aubrey Boesak and Curtis Paul DeYoung. Maryknoll: N.Y.: Orbis, 2013, p. 107.
10. Thich Nhat Hanh. *Awakening of the Heart: Essential Buddhist Sutras and Commentaries*. Berkeley: Parallax, 2012, p. 144.
11. Michelle Alexander. *The New Jim Crow: Mass Incarceration in the Age of Colorblindness*. New York: New Press, 2012.
12. bell hooks. "Buddhism and the Politics of Domination," in *Mindful Politics: A Buddhist Guide to Making the World a Better Place* edited by Melvin McLeod. Boston: Wisdom, 2006, p. 60.
13. Jack Kornfield. *Bringing Home the Dharma*. Boston: Shambhala, 2011.
14. King. *Strength to Love, op. cit.*, p. 33.
15. Alistair Boddy-Evans. "More Quotes: Nelson Mandela" <http://africanhistory.about.com/od/mandelanelson/p/qts_mandela2.htm>.
16. Elie Wiesel. *The Night Trilogy*. New York: Hill and Wang, 2008, p. 13.
17. Howard Thurman, "Reconciliation," in *A Strange Freedom: The Best of Howard Thurman on Religious Experience and Public Life* edited by Walter Earl Fluker and Catherine Tumber. Boston: Beacon, 1998, p. 183.
18. Charles Johnson. *Turning the Wheel*. New York: Scribner, 2003, p. 46.
19. King. *Strength to Love, op. cit.*, pp. 47–48.
20. Jon Kabat-Zinn. *Wherever You Go, There You Are: Mindfulness Meditation in Everyday Life*. New York: Hyperion, 2005, p. 49.

21. Howard Thurman. "Religion in a Time of Crisis," in Fluker and Tumber, *op cit.*, p. 128.

Chapter 3: Extend Compassion, Love, and Kindness to Those Who Express and Act with Ill Will

1. Hafiz. "We Have Not Come to Take Prisoners," in *The Gift: Poems by Hafiz, The Great Sufi Master,* translated by Daniel Ladinsky. New York: Penguin, 1999, p. 28.
2. Prachi Gupta. "GOP Official Resigns Over Racist 'Daily Show' Interview," Salon.com, October 24, 2013.
3. "Anti-Gay Hate Crimes Set to Double in New York City in 2013" Rt.com, August 19, 2013.
4. Thich Nhat Hanh. *Going Home: Jesus and Buddha as Brothers.* New York: Riverhead, 1999, p. 165.
5. Martin Luther King, Jr. "Nonviolence and Racial Justice," in *A Testament of Hope: The Essential Writings and Speeches of Martin Luther King Jr.* edited by James M. Washington. San Francisco: Harper, 1986, p. 8.
6. Howard Thurman. "Reconciliation," in *A Strange Freedom: The Best of Howard Thurman on Religious Experience and Public Life* edited by Walter Earl Fluker and Catherine Tumber. Boston: Beacon, 1998, p. 170.
7. *A Course in Miracles: The Advent of a Great Awakening*. New York: Barnes & Noble, 2007, p. 259.
8. Pema Chödrön. *The Places That Scare You: A Guide to Fearlessness in Difficult Times*. Boston: Shambhala, 2001, p. 50.
9. Associated Press. "'His Story Must Not Be Forgotten.'" Politico.com, March 31, 2013 <http://www.politico.com/story/2013/03/elwin-wilson-death-89498.html>.
10. Congressman John Lewis (2013). "Rep. John Lewis Saddened by Passing of Elwin Wilson, Rock Hill Man Who Apologized." Press release, April 2, 2013.

11. James Baldwin. *The Price of the Ticket: Collected Nonfiction, 1948–1985*. New York: St. Martin's, 1985, p. 145.
12. *Ibid.*, p. 138.
13. Lewis, *op cit.*
14. Jack Kornfield, *After the Ecstasy, the Laundry*, New York: Bantam, 2000, p. 69.
15. Bob Marley, "Coming in from the Cold," on *Uprising*. Kingston, Jamaica: Tuff Gong, 1980.
16. "Nelson Mandela Quotes: A Collection of Memorable Words from Former South African President," CBSNews.com, December 5, 2013 <http://www.cbsnews.com/news/nelson-mandela-quotes-a-collection-of-memorable-words-from-former-south-african-president/>.
17. "Ex-Klansman Elwin Wilson 'I'm Sorry.'" CNN story, with Don Lemon. YouTube video, posted February 8, 2009 <http://www.youtube.com/watch?v=sTKEokcd8M4>.
18. Lewis. *op cit.*
19. Martin Luther King, Jr. *Strength to Love*, Minneapolis: Fortress, 2010, pp. 46–47.
20. H. H. the Dalai Lama. *Beyond Religion: Ethics for a Whole World*. Boston: Mariner Books, 2012, p. 128.
21. Hanh. *Going Home*, *op cit.*, p. 164.
22. H. H. the Dalai Lama. *Beyond Religion*, *op cit.*, p. 129.
23. H. H. the Dalai Lama. Unsourced.
24. Thurman. "Reconciliation," in Fluker and Tumber, *op cit.*, pp. 172–73.
25. Joseph Goldstein. "Three Means to Peace," in *Mindful Politics: A Buddhist Guide to Making the World a Better Place* edited by Melvin McLeod. Boston: Wisdom, 2006, pp. 124–25.
26. Martin Luther King Jr. *Why We Can't Wait*. New York: New American Library, 2000, p. 24.
27. Quoted in Kornfield. *After the Ecstasy, the Laundry*, *op cit.*, p. 225.
28. Khalil Gibran. "Sand and Foam," in *The Garden of the Prophet, Lazarus and His Beloved*. Middlesex: Echo Library, 2009, p. 22.

29. King. "Pilgrimage to Nonviolence," in Washington, *op cit.*, p. 39.
30. *Ibid.*
31. *A Course in Miracles*, *op cit.*, p. 316.
32. Thurman. "Reconciliation," in Fluker and Tumber, *op cit.*, p. 181.
33. Lewis. *op cit.*

Chapter 4: Reestablish a Connection to Earth

1. Martin Luther King, Jr. *Strength to Love*, Minneapolis: Fortress, 2010, p. 69.
2. Alice Walker, "This Was Not an Area of Large Plantations: Suffering Too Insignificant for the Majority to See," in *Dharma, Color and Culture: New Voices in Western Buddhism* edited by Hilda Gutiérrez Baldoquin. Berkeley: Parallax, 2004, p. 191.
3. Martin Luther King, Jr. "An Experiment in Love" in *A Testament of Hope: The Essential Writings and Speeches of Martin Luther King Jr.* edited by James M. Washington. San Francisco: Harper, 1986, p. 19.
4. *Ibid.*
5. "I visited all quarters with my mind // Nor found I any dearer than myself; // Self is likewise to every other dear; // Who loves himself will never harm another." Quoted in Donald Rothberg. *The Engaged Spiritual Life: A Buddhist Approach to Transforming Ourselves and the World*. Boston: Beacon, 2006, p. 103.
6. Quoted in Sharon Salzberg, *Lovingkindness: The Revolutionary Art of Happiness*. Boston: Shambhala, 2002, p. 119.
7. *A Course in Miracles: The Advent of a Great Awakening*. New York: Barnes & Noble, 2007, p. 177.
8. In his 1964 Nobel Peace Prize lecture, for instance, King wrote that "in the final analysis, the rich must not ignore the poor because both rich and poor are tied in a single garment of destiny. All life is interrelated, and all men are interdependent. The agony of the poor diminishes the rich, and the salvation of the poor enlarges the rich.

We are inevitably our brothers' keeper because of the interrelated structure of reality." See <http://www.nobelprize.org/nobel_prizes/peace/laureates/1964/king-lecture.html>. We find this sentiment again expressed in King's 1967 "Christmas Sermon on Peace": "It really boils down to this: that all life is interrelated. We are all caught in an inescapable network of mutuality, tied into a single garment of destiny. Whatever affects one directly, affects all indirectly. We are made to live together because of the interrelated structure of reality." See Washington, *A Testament of Hope*, *op cit.*, p. 254. Martin Luther King, Jr. included the statement, too, in his "Letter from a Birmingham City Jail," in *Why We Can't Wait*. New York: New American Library, 2000, p. 65. These are only a few examples of where the statement "all life is interrelated" appears.

9. King, *Why We Can't Wait, op cit.*, p. 142.
10. Howard Thurman. "Excerpt from 'The Luminous Darkness,'" in *A Strange Freedom: The Best of Howard Thurman on Religious Experience and Public Life* edited by Walter Earl Fluker and Catherine Tumber. Boston: Beacon, 1998, p. 245.
11. "Karaniya Metta Sutta: The Buddha's Words of Loving-Kindness," translated from the Pali by the Amaravati Sangha, 2004 <http://www.accesstoinsight.org/tipitaka/kn/snp/snp.1.08.amar.html>.
12. Thich Nhat Hanh. "The Sun My Heart," in *Engaged Buddhist Reader* edited by Arnold Kotler. Berkeley: Parallax Press, 1996, p. 164.
13. Michael Starkey. "Wilderness, Race, and African Americans: An Environmental History from Slavery to Jim Crow," (2005) M.A. thesis, University of California, Berkeley, 2005, p. 32 <http://goo.gl/71XMOy>.
14. La Familia Verde Urban Farms, a community farm located in the Bronx, New York, is a great case in point. Here, residents not only produce food for the local community but also provide a healthy gathering place where folks can learn gardening and other skills that reconnect them to the natural environment. See Daphne Miller, M.D. *Farmacology*. New York: HarperCollins, 2013, pp. 163–92.

15. Alice Walker. *The Color Purple*. New York: Pocket, 1982, pp. 178–79.
16. "Principles of Environmental Justice" <http://www.ejnet.org/ej/principles.html>. At the First National People of Color Environmental Leadership Summit, held on September 27, 1991, "delegates adopted 17 principles of environmental justice. Since then, *The Principles* have served as the defining document for the growing grassroots movement for environmental justice."
17. Mart A. Stewart. "Slavery and the Origins of African American Environmentalism," in *"To Love the Wind and the Rain": African Americans and Environmental History* edited by Dianne D. Glave and Mark Stoll. Pittsburgh: University of Pittsburgh, 2006, p. 17.
18. William Wordsworth. "The World Is Too Much with Us" (1807) <http://www.poetryfoundation.org/poem/174833>.
19. Cassandra Y. Johnson and Josh McDaniel. "Turpentine Negro," in Glave and Stoll, *op cit.*, p. 52.
20. Mireya Navarro. "National Parks Reach Out to Blacks Who Aren't Visiting," *New York Times*, November 2, 2010.
21. Melissa Harris-Perry. "Michael Vick, Racial History and Animal Rights," *The Nation*, December 20, 2010.
22. Navarro, *op cit.*
23. This chant is based on Thich Nhat Hanh's guided meditation "Touching the Earth."
24. Hanh. "The Sun My Heart," in Kotler, *op cit.*, p. 165.
25. Johnson and McDaniel. "Turpentine Negro," in Glave and Stoll, *op cit.*, p. 62.
26. Colin Fisher. "African Americans, Outdoor Recreation, and the 1919 Chicago Race Riot," in Glave and Stoll, *op cit.*, p. 76.
27. Alice Walker. Foreword to Marjorie Spiegel's *The Dreaded Comparison: Animal Slavery and Human Slavery*. New York: Mirror/IDEA, 1997, p. 14.
28. Salzberg. *Lovingkindness*, *op cit.*, p. 174.
29. King. *Why We Can't Wait*, *op cit.*, pp. 33–34.

Chapter 5: Strive to Be in Good Bodily Health

1. Quoted in *Sistah Vegan: Black Female Vegans Speak on Food, Identity, Health, and Society* edited by A. Breeze Harper. New York: Lantern, 2010, p. 21.
2. Howard Thurman. "Reconciliation," in *A Strange Freedom: The Best of Howard Thurman on Religious Experience and Public Life* edited by Walter Earl Fluker and Catherine Tumber. Boston: Beacon, 1998, p. 177.
3. "According to the U.S. Department of Labor (2012) coffee is produced with forced labor in Côte D'Ivoire (CDI) and with child labor in Colombia, CDI, Dominican Republic, Guatemala, Guinea, Honduras, El Salvador, Kenya, Mexico, Nicaragua, Panama, Sierra Leone, Tanzania, and Uganda. Other reports have found forced labor throughout Latin America, particularly in those countries that the Department of Labor has identified as using child labor." See Verité: Fair Labor. Worldwide. *Coffee,* <http://www.verite.org/Commodities/Coffee>.
4. "The Five Mindfulness Trainings," from Deer Park Monastery in the Great Hidden Mountain <http://deerparkmonastery.org/mindfulness-practice/the-five-mindfulness-trainings>. These trainings are conceived of as the "concrete expression of the Buddha's teachings on the Four Noble Truths and the Noble Eightfold Path." Through the first four trainings that Thich Nhat Hanh outlines, the layperson develops habits of mind that reinforce a commitment to protect the lives of all sentient beings, to cultivate generosity, to act with integrity in matters of sexuality, and to practice wise and thoughtful speech as well as listening. And the fifth is the practitioner's express commitment to exercise great care in what she chooses to consume, i.e., what she takes into her body as well as her mind.
5. The Buddha's precepts, translated from Pali, read: "For the sake of training, I undertake the precept to abstain from the taking of life. // For the sake of training, I undertake the precept not to take that which is not given. // For the sake of training, I undertake the

precept to abstain from sexual misconduct. // For the sake of the training, I undertake the precept to abstain from unwise speech. // For the sake of the training, I undertake the precept to abstain from intoxicants that cause heedlessness." Quoted in Donald Rothberg. *The Engaged Spiritual Life: A Buddhist Approach to Transforming Ourselves and the World.* Boston: Beacon, 2006, p. 10.

6. Indeed, "livestock production accounts for 18 percent of global greenhouse gas emissions, including 9 percent of carbon dioxide and 37 percent of methane gas emissions worldwide." See "Consequences of Increased Global Meat Consumption on the Global Environment—Trade in Virtual Water, Energy & Nutrients," by Cassandra Brooks. Stanford Woods Institute for the Environment <https://woods.stanford.edu/environmental-venture-projects/consequences-increased-global-meat-consumption-global-environment>.
7. Adama Maweja. "The Fulfillment of the Movement," in Harper, *op cit.*, p. 135.
8. Martin Luther King, Jr. "Christmas Sermon on Peace," in *A Testament of Hope: The Essential Writings and Speeches of Martin Luther King Jr.* edited by James M. Washington. San Francisco: Harper, 1986, p. 254.
9. Felicity Lawrence. "Omega-3, Junk Food and the Link between Violence and What We Eat," *Guardian,* October 17, 2006.
10. A. Breeze Harper. "Social Justice Beliefs and Addiction to Uncompassionate Consumption: Food for Thought," in Harper, *op cit.*, p. 39.
11. Maweja, *op cit.*, p. 135.
12. Charles Johnson, "Reading the Eightfold Path," in *Dharma, Color and Culture: New Voices in Western Buddhism* edited by Hilda Gutiérrez Baldoquin. Berkeley: Parallax, 2004, p. 138.
13. Allan Aubrey Boesak, *Dare We Speak of Hope? Searching for a Language of Life in Faith and Politics.* Grand Rapids: Eerdmans, 2014, p.118.

Chapter 6: Cultivate Hope

1. Melissa Santosa. "Identity, Freedom, and Veganism," in *Sistah Vegan: Black Female Vegans Speak on Food, Identity, Health, and Society* edited by A. Breeze Harper. New York: Lantern, 2010, p. 77.
2. "James W. Stewart," in *Foot Soldiers for Democracy: The Men, Women, and Children of the Birmingham Civil Rights Movement* edited by Horace Huntley and John W. McKerley. Chicago and Urbana: University of Illinois Press, 2009, p. 138.
3. Allan Aubrey Boesak, *Dare We Speak of Hope? Searching for a Language of Life in Faith and Politics*. Grand Rapids: Eerdmans, 2014, p. 4.
4. Martin Luther King, Jr. "Letter from a Birmingham City Jail," in *A Testament of Hope: The Essential Writings and Speeches of Martin Luther King Jr.* edited by James M. Washington. San Francisco: Harper, 1986, p. 293.
5. Quoted from Governor George Wallace's inaugural address, given on January 14, 1963. See "George Wallace, Segregation Symbol, Dies at 79," Howell Raines, *New York Times*, September 14, 1998.
6. Martin Luther King, Jr. *Why We Can't Wait*, New York: New American Library, 2000, p. 36.
7. Charles Johnson. *Turning the Wheel.* New York: Scribner, 2003, p. 46.
8. Frederick Douglass. "Narrative of the Life of Frederick Douglass," in *The Norton Anthology of African American Literature* edited by Henry Louis Gates Jr. and Nellie Y. McKay. New York: W. W. Norton, 1997, p. 336.
9. *Ibid.*, p. 339.
10. *Ibid.*
11. "James Roberson," in Huntley and McKerley, *op cit.*, p. 114.
12. Patricia J. Williams. *The Alchemy of Race and Rights*. Cambridge: Harvard University Press, 1991, p. 73.

13. Parker J. Palmer. *A Hidden Wholeness: The Journey Toward an Undivided Life*. San Francisco: Jossey-Bass, 2004, p. 169.
14. Parker J. Palmer. *Healing the Heart of Democracy*. San Francisco: Jossey-Bass, 2011, p. 7.
15. Williams. *op. cit.*, p. 73.
16. Palmer. *A Hidden Wholeness, op cit.*, p. 169.
17. Boesak. *Dare We Speak of Hope? op. cit.*, p. 8.
18. "Emma Smith Young," in Huntley and McKerley, *op. cit.*, p. 5.
19. Boesak. *Dare We Speak of Hope? op. cit.*, pp. 26–27.
20. Allan Aubrey Boesak. "Reconciliation, Risk and Resistance: The Story of Rizpah," in *Radical Reconciliation: Beyond Political Pietism and Christian Quietism* by Allan Aubrey Boesak and Curtis Paul DeYoung. Maryknoll: N.Y.: Orbis, 2013, p. 38.
21. 134 S. Ct. 1623, 1676 (2014).
22. "Language can indeed create hope out of nothing, can cause hope to flourish, if it is spoken to be life-giving and life-affirming. But then, it has to be a new language. The old language of our colonized and crippled minds, the language of fear and trepidation, of unbelief and cynicism, of ignorance and resignation, of internalized inferiorities and externalized submissiveness, cannot produce a new language. Hope is the language of life because it exposes the truth about life. It dislodges and replaces not just the language but also the logic of oppression." Boesak. *Dare We Speak of Hope? op. cit.*, pp. 25–26.
23. "Eva Lou Billingsley Russell," in Huntley and McKerley, *op. cit.*, p. 13. Carlton Reese was director of the ACHMR choir. He composed many of the now-famous civil rights movement songs.
24. Boesak. *Dare We Speak of Hope? op. cit.*, p. 27.
25. "Henry M. Goodgame Sr.," in Huntley and McKerley, *op cit.*, p. 61.
26. Boesak. *Dare We Speak of Hope? op. cit.*, p. 139.
27. Joe Volk. "Practicing Hope, Way Opens: Wilmington College Commencement Address," Friends Committee on National

Legislation, May 7, 2011 <http://fcnl.org/about/who/staff/writings/practicing_hope_way_opens/>.

28. Boesak. "Reconciliation," in Boesak and DeYoung, *op. cit.*, p. 37.
29. King. "I See the Promised Land," in Washington, *op cit.*, p. 286.
30. Peter Gabel. "Law and Economics, Critical Legal Studies, and the Higher Law: Critical Legal Studies as a Spiritual Practice," 36 *Pepp. L. Rev.* 515, 521 (2009). My emphasis.
31. "The Five Mindfulness Trainings," from Deer Park Monastery in the Great Hidden Mountain <http://deerparkmonastery.org/mindfulness-practice/the-five-mindfulness-trainings>.
32. Jan Willis. "A Peaceful World Begins with Small Peaceful Actions," in *Mindful Politics: A Buddhist Guide to Making the World a Better Place* edited by Melvin McLeod. Boston: Wisdom, 2006, p. 108.
33. Boesak. *Dare We Speak of Hope?, op cit.*, p. 168.
34. *Ibid.*, p. 19.
35. *Ibid.*, p. 16.

Conclusion

1. "The Instruction to the Kalamas: Anguttara Nikaya, Tika Nipata, Mahavagga, Sutta no. 65. Translated from the Pali by Soma Thera and alternatively by Thanissaro Bhikkhu" <http://web.ics.purdue.edu/~buddhism/docs/KalamaSutta.pdf>.
2. A. B. Spelman and Malcolm X. "Interview with Malcolm X," *Monthly Review*, vol 56, issue February 9, 2005. The interview was conducted on March 19, 1964 <http://monthlyreview.org/2005/02/01/interview-with-malcolm-x>.
3. George Jackson. *Soledad Brother.* Chicago: Lawrence Hill, 1994, p. 224.
4. Huey P. Newton. *Revolutionary Suicide.* New York: Penguin, 2009, p. 115.
5. "Annetta Streeter Gary," in *Foot Soldiers for Democracy: The Men, Women, and Children of the Birmingham Civil Rights Movement*

edited by Horace Huntley and John W. McKerley. Chicago and Urbana: University of Illinois Press, 2009, p. 121.

6. June Jordan. *Some of Us Did Not Die: New and Selected Essays*. New York: Basic, 2002, p. 44.
7. Martin Luther King, Jr. "Nonviolence: The Only Road to Freedom," in *A Testament of Hope: The Essential Writings and Speeches of Martin Luther King Jr.* edited by James M. Washington. San Francisco: Harper, 1986, p. 58.
8. Nonviolent resistance has actually been more successful than generally assumed. See Erica Chenoweth and Maria J. Stephan. *Why Civil Resistance Works: The Strategic Logic of Nonviolent Conflict*. New York: Columbia University, 2011.
9. Barry L. Gan. *Violence and Nonviolence: An Introduction*. Lanham, Md.: Rowman & Littlefield, 2013, p. 41.
10. Allan Aubrey Boesak, *Dare We Speak of Hope? : Searching for a Language of Life in Faith and Politics*. Grand Rapids: Eerdmans, 2014, p. 116.
11. This quote is from Vice President Joe Biden's speech following the ISIS beheading of journalists Steven Sotloff and James Foley. "Biden Talks Gates of Hell; Seeking Clues in Beheading Videos; ISIS Caliphate." *Transcripts, CNN Newsroom*, aired September 3, 2014 <http://transcripts.cnn.com/TRANSCRIPTS/1409/03/cnr.05.html>.
12. King. "A Time to Break Silence," in Washington, *op cit.*, p. 233.
13. Martin Luther King, Jr. *Why We Can't Wait*, New York: New American Library, 2000, p. 143.
14. From "Poem for South Africa," in *Directed by Desire: The Collected Poems of June Jordan.* Port Townsend, Wash.: Copper Canyon, 2007, p. 278.

#bibliography

Alexander, Michelle. *The New Jim Crow: Mass Incarceration in the Age of Colorblindness*. New York: New Press, 2012.

Baldoquin, Hilda Gutiérrez (ed). *Dharma, Color and Culture: New Voices in Western Buddhism*. Berkeley: Parallax Press, 2004.

Baldwin, James. *The Price of the Ticket: Collected Nonfiction, 1948–1985*. New York: St. Martin's, 1985.

Beckwith, Michael Bernard. *Spiritual Liberation: Fulfilling Your Soul's Potential*. New York: ATRIA, 2008.

Boesak, Allan Aubrey. *Dare We Speak of Hope? Searching for a Language of Life in Faith and Politics*. Grand Rapids: Eerdmans, 2014.

Boesak, Allan Aubrey, and Curtis Paul DeYoung. *Radical Reconciliation: Beyond Political Pietism and Christian Quietism*. Maryknoll: N.Y.: Orbis, 2013.

Chenoweth, Erica, and Maria J. Stephan. *Why Civil Resistance Works: The Strategic Logic of Nonviolent Conflict*. New York: Columbia University Press, 2011.

Chödrön, Pema. *The Places that Scare You: A Guide to Fearlessness in Difficult Times*. Boston: Shambhala, 2001.

Course in Miracles, A: The Advent of a Great Awakening. New York: Barnes & Noble, 2007.

Dalai Lama, H. H. *Beyond Religion: Ethics for a Whole World*. Boston: Mariner, 2012.

Fluker, Walter Earl, and Catherine Tumber (eds). *A Strange Freedom: The Best of Howard Thurman on Religious Experience and Public Life*. Boston: Beacon Press, 1998.

Gan, Barry L. *Violence and Nonviolence: An Introduction*. Lanham, Md.: Rowman & Littlefield, 2013.

Gates, Henry Louis, and Nellie Y. McKay (eds). *The Norton Anthology of African American Literature*. New York: W. W. Norton, 1997.

Gibran, Khalil. *The Garden of the Prophet, Lazarus and His Beloved*. Middlesex: Echo Library, 2009. Glave, Dianne D., and Mark Stoll (eds). *"To Love the Wind and the Rain": African Americans and Environmental History*. Pittsburgh: University of Pittsburgh, 2006.

Hafiz. *The Gift: Poems by Hafiz, The Great Sufi Master,* translated by Daniel Ladinsky. New York: Penguin, 1999.

Hanh, Thich Nhat. *Awakening of the Heart: Essential Buddhist Sutras and Commentaries*. Berkeley: Parallax, 2012.

——. *Going Home: Jesus and Buddha as Brothers*. New York: Riverhead, 1999.

Harper, A. Breeze (ed). *Sistah Vegan: Black Female Vegans Speak on Food, Identity, Health, and Society*. New York: Lantern, 2010.

Huntley, Horace, and John W. McKerley, (eds). *Foot Soldiers for Democracy: The Men, Women, and Children of the Birmingham Civil Rights Movement*. Chicago and Urbana: University of Illinois, 2009.

Jackson, George. *Soledad Brother*. Chicago: Lawrence Hill, 1994.

Johnson, Charles. *Turning the Wheel*. New York: Scribner, 2003.

Jordan, June. *Directed by Desire: The Collected Poems of June Jordan*. Port Townsend, Wash.: Copper Canyon, 2007.

——. *Some of Us Did Not Die: New and Selected Essays*. New York: Basic, 2002.

Kabat-Zinn, Jon. *Wherever You Go, There You Are: Mindfulness Meditation in Everyday Life*. New York: Hyperion, 2005.

King Jr., Martin Luther. *Strength to Love*. Minneapolis: Fortress, 2010.

——. *Why We Can't Wait*. New York: New American Library, 2000.

Kornfield, Jack. *After the Ecstasy, the Laundry*. New York: Bantam, 2000.

——. *Bringing Home the Dharma*. Boston: Shambhala, 2011.

Kotler, Arnold (ed). *Engaged Buddhist Reader*. Berkeley: Parallax, 1996.

Lorde, Audre. *Sister Outsider*. Trumansburg, N.Y.: Crossing, 1984.

McLeod, Melvin (ed). *Mindful Politics: A Buddhist Guide to Making the World a Better Place*. Boston: Wisdom Publications, 2006.

Newton, Huey P. *Revolutionary Suicide*. New York: Penguin, 2009.

Palmer, Parker J. *Healing the Heart of Democracy*. San Francisco: Jossey-Bass, 2011.

——. *A Hidden Wholeness: The Journey toward an Undivided Life*. San Francisco: Jossey-Bass, 2004.

Rothberg, Donald. *The Engaged Spiritual Life: A Buddhist Approach to Transforming Ourselves and the World*. Boston: Beacon, 2006.

Salzberg, Sharon. *Lovingkindness: The Revolutionary Art of Happiness*. Boston: Shambhala, 2002.

Sampson, Anthony. *Mandela: The Authorized Biography*. New York: Vintage, 1999.

Spiegel, Marjorie. *The Dreaded Comparison: Animal Slavery and Human Slavery*. New York: Mirror Books/IDEA, 1997.

Still, William. *The Underground Railroad: Authentic Narratives and First-hand Accounts*. Mineola, N.Y.: Dover, 2007.

Walker, Alice. *The Color Purple*. New York: Pocket, 1982.

Washington, James M. (ed). *A Testament of Hope: The Essential Writings and Speeches of Martin Luther King Jr.* San Francisco: Harper, 1986.

Wiesel, Elie. *The Night Trilogy*. New York: Hill and Wang, 2008.

Williams, Patricia. J. *The Alchemy of Race and Rights*. Cambridge: Harvard University, 1991.

About the Publisher

LANTERN BOOKS was founded in 1999 on the principle of living with a greater depth and commitment to the preservation of the natural world. In addition to publishing books on animal advocacy, vegetarianism, religion, and environmentalism, Lantern is dedicated to printing books in the United States on recycled paper and saving resources in day-to-day operations. Lantern is honored to be a recipient of the highest standard in environmentally responsible publishing from the Green Press Initiative.

www.lanternbooks.com